Deliberation on the Cause of the Poor

SOURCES IN EARLY MODERN ECONOMICS, ETHICS, AND LAW

Second Series

GENERAL EDITORS

Andrew M. McGinnis
Junius Institute • USA

Wim Decock
UCLouvain and ULiège • Belgium

Continuing in the line of its predecessor, this series publishes original English translations and editions of early modern religious texts in the disciplines of economics, ethics, and law. Representing a variety of confessional traditions and methodological approaches, these texts uncover the foundations of the development of these and related disciplines.

EDITORIAL BOARD

Jordan J. Ballor
Center for Religion, Culture & Democracy • USA

Christiane Birr
Max Planck Institute for European Legal History • Germany

Stephen Bogle
University of Glasgow • Scotland

Alejandro Chafuen
Acton Institute • USA

Ricardo F. Crespo
Universidad Austral and CONICET • Argentina

Virpi Mäkinen
University of Helsinki • Finland

Richard A. Muller
Calvin Theological Seminary • USA

Herman Selderhuis
Theological University Apeldoorn • The Netherlands

John Witte Jr.
Emory University • USA

Zhibin Xie
Tongji University • China

Deliberation on the Cause of the Poor

Domingo de Soto

Edited by Wim Decock
Translated by Joost Possemiers and Jeremiah Lasquety-Reyes
Introduction by Daniel Schwartz

GRAND RAPIDS · MICHIGAN

Deliberation on the Cause of the Poor

Translation © 2022 by Joost Possemiers and Jeremiah Lasquety-Reyes

Introduction © 2022 by Daniel Schwartz

All rights reserved. No part of this publication may be reproduced, stored in a retrieval system, or transmitted in any form or by any means, including electronic, mechanical, photocopying, recording, or otherwise without the prior permission of the publisher.

ISBN 978-1-949011-09-8 (hardcover)
ISBN 978-1-949011-10-4 (paperback)
ISBN 978-1-949011-11-1 (ebook)

C L P Academic
 *An imprint of the Acton Institute
 for the Study of Religion & Liberty*
98 E. Fulton
Grand Rapids, Michigan 49503
616.454.3080
www.acton.org

Interior composition by Judy Schafer
Cover design by Scaturro Design

Contents

Acknowledgments	*vii*
Introduction	*ix*
Translators' Note	*xlv*
Abbreviations	*xlix*

Deliberation on the Cause of the Poor

To the Reader	3
1. Dedicatory Epistle	5
2. Outline of the Events	11
3. On Vagabonds	17
4. On Foreign Beggars	27
5. Refutation of the Objections	39
6. The Pilgrims to Saint James	45
7. The Final End of the Plan for the Poor	49
8. The Obligation by Which Christians Are Bound to Give Alms	59
9. The Examination of the Poverty of the Beggars	67
10. The Evaluation of the Life of the Poor	77
11. On the Manner of Asking from Door to Door	93
12. Weighing the Reasons and Arguments to Prohibit the Poor from Begging	115
Index	127

Acknowledgments

Charity, compassion, and care for the poor are at the heart of the biblical tradition, with the gospel reinforcing Old Testament texts on the necessity of alleviating the plight of the needy.[1] Yet how Judeo-Christian principles should translate into practice has been the subject of incessant debate. While Christian communities in the late Roman Empire started building poorhouses, orphanages, elderly homes and guesthouses for foreigners, the question remained who, exactly, could qualify as poor and needy. In the medieval canon law tradition, a distinction was drawn between the deserving and the undeserving poor, or between legitimate and illegitimate beggars. Furthermore, conflicts arose between spiritual and temporal authorities when deciding who should be in charge of the policies and practices of poor relief. Both bishops and princes considered themselves as heirs to the power of Roman emperors to protect the poor, pursuant to provisions in Justinian's Code about procedural privileges granted to so-called "miserable persons" (Cod. 3.14). Tensions came to a head in the early sixteenth century when the argument that laypeople and temporal governments should organize poor relief, not clerics and bishops, received decisive intellectual support from humanists such as Juan Luis Vives and Protestant theologians following Martin Luther's teachings on the public nature of poor relief.

---

[1] Gary A. Anderson, *Charity: The Place of the Poor in the Biblical Tradition* (New Haven, CT: Yale University Press, 2014).

Acknowledgments

Domingo de Soto's *Deliberation on the Cause of the Poor*, first published in Salamanca in 1545, stands out as a major witness to the early modern controversy on poor relief. Unhappy with the foundation of public welfare institutions in Flemish, German, and Castilian cities as well as legislative attempts by Emperor Charles V to make it harder for outside beggars to access social assistance, Soto ventured into a defense of genuinely poor people moving from one place to another and appealing to private charity. At the same time, he defended the church's role in providing moral and religious incentives to the rich to relieve the plight of the poor through almsgiving practices. Voicing conservative concerns, Soto was worried about the fact that even among Catholics the idea had gained ground that a more efficient approach against begging and vagrancy required the involvement of lay experts and temporal authorities. He resented the policy of granting annual licenses to the legitimate poor who were subject to medical examination, interrogation, and receipt of the sacraments of confession and communion. Soto feared not only abuse of the sacraments but also violation of the natural and divine rights of poor people.

A first glimpse of Soto's seminal contribution to the debate on poverty relief was offered to me at the International School of Ius Commune in Erice in October 2013. Without the invitation of Manlio Bellomo, Orazio Condorelli, and Ken Pennington to participate in the thirty-third course on "Social crisis and science of law in the medieval and modern world," my interest in Soto's *Deliberation* would not have been raised in the first place. I am grateful to Joost Possemiers and Jeremiah Lasquety-Reyes for having accepted the difficult task of rendering Soto's Latin text into English. They have risen to the challenge and, despite the rather arid and abstract character of Soto's style, have succeeded in offering a smooth English translation of the *In causa pauperum deliberatio*. Part of the translation work was funded through the Heinz Maier-Leibnitz Prize awarded to me in 2014 while I was still a research group leader at the Max-Planck-Institute for Legal History and Legal Theory in Frankfurt. I would also like to extend my gratitude to Daniel Schwartz for his willingness to write the introduction to this volume. His unique expertise on sociopolitical thought in early modern Spain will serve as an excellent guide.

— Wim Decock

Introduction*

Daniel Schwartz

The *Deliberation*

Domingo de Soto's *Deliberation on the Cause of the Poor* is the most thorough and incisive piece of criticism against the reform of poor laws in sixteenth-century Europe. Soto's essay can be read as a warning about the darker sides of what could be considered to be a precursory welfare state. These darker sides comprise the exclusion of the poor from the public space, their forced institutional seclusion, and violations of their privacy through their subjection to humiliating examinations that often turned them into objects of curiosity for the wealthy.

Soto's main concern about the new poor relief laws is that they confound justice and mercy by making people's eligibility to receive alms conditional not only on their being law-abiding citizens but also—more ambitiously—on their being morally decent and good Christians.[1] True mercy is about the unconditional alleviation of our neighbor's need, no questions asked.[2] Soto insists that mercy should not be dena-

---

* I would like to acknowledge the generous help of Wim Decock in making comments, suggestions, and corrections, as well as María Pilar Domingo Cuesta, Stephen Gaetano, Héctor Linares, Santiago Orrego, Alberto Octavio Partida Gómez, Armando Pavón Romero, Joost Possemiers, Francisco Vicente Navarro, Naly Thaler, and Marco Toste.

[1] Domingo de Soto, *In causa pauperum deliberatio*, ed. Jaime Brufau Prats, in Soto, *Relecciones y opúsculos*, II-2 (Salamanca: San Esteban, 2011), VII, 131–35 (p. 268); IX, 15–20 (p. 281).

[2] Soto, *Deliberatio*, X, 33 (p. 296).

tured by making it into a vehicle for pursuing other ends, worthy as they may be. The confounding of mercy and justice distorts the right social division of moral work: justice should be the business of state-appointed officials and mercy of all private citizens. However, under the new proposals, says Soto, magistrates coercively enforce duties of charity. The duty to give alms lies beyond what he takes to be the state magistrates' legitimate coercive scope, which consists for him in the enforcement of justice alone.[3]

According to Soto, the new laws enable the state to overstep its limits in an additional respect. By conditioning the eligibility of poor people for assistance on an examination of their sins, these laws in effect give to justice officials the prerogative to punish, by withholding such assistance, sins that are not punishable under the law. Such sins belong to the confessional and will be divinely punished in the next life.[4] The new laws not only enable state officials to punish what is not for them to punish but also to punish unfairly by targeting only some of the guilty, namely, only that part of the population who are in need of relief.[5]

The Life of Domingo de Soto

The best and most complete biography of Domingo de Soto, despite its panegyric tone and frequent digressions, remains Vicente Beltrán de Heredia's monumental *Domingo de Soto: Estudio biográfico docu-*

---

[3] For example, in *De iustitia et iure*, 5.1.7 (p. 400), Soto argues that the state should restrict itself to enforcing justice and does not have the competence to enforce charitable duties. If people are in great necessity, he says, we have a duty to give them alms but cannot be coerced to do so by the state. Soto, *De iustitia et iure libri decem* (1556), ed. Venancio Diego Carro and P. Marcelino González Ordóñez, 5 vols. (Madrid: Instituto de Estudios Políticos, 1968).

[4] Soto, *Deliberatio*, IX, 170–75 (p. 290).

[5] Soto, *Deliberatio*, VII, 130–35 (p. 268); IX, 30–35 (p. 282), 165–70 (pp. 289–90).

mentado.⁶ What follows is no more than a summary of some of the main events in Soto's life.

Born in Segovia in 1495 to a family of farmers of modest means, the son of Pablo de Arévalo and Catalina de Soto, Francisco de Soto was around fifteen years old when he left for the recently created University of Alcalá. He began the arts course in 1513. Around 1516, after graduating as bachelor in arts, Soto left for Paris, where Francisco de Vitoria was also studying. Soto was accepted to the Collège Sainte-Barbe and studied theology for at least two years. He may also have taken classes with the nominalist John Mair at the Collège de Montaigu.

Soto returned to Alcalá in the first months of the academic year 1519–1520, joining his lifelong friend Pedro Fernández de Saavedra at the Colegio de San Ildefonso and continuing his theology courses under Pedro Ciruelo. By 1523 or 1524, Soto met the requirements for receiving a degree in theology. But instead of asking for his degree, he decided to change course: he would abandon secular life and join a religious order. He headed to Montserrat to join the Benedictines. However, "a very old and wise friar" persuaded him that his talents would be put to better use with the Order of the Preachers.[7] So Soto headed to the Convent of San Pablo in Burgos where he made his profession on July 23, 1524, and took the name "Domingo." He moved to the Convent of San Esteban at Salamanca in 1525 with the intention to apply for a chair in theology. Made *magister* and licensed under the patronage of the major figure of the School of Salamanca, Francisco de Vitoria, in 1531 Soto applied for and obtained the Salamanca Chair of Vespers (the afternoon class). Soto held this post for sixteen years, teaching mainly on the basis of Aquinas's *Summa* and the *Sentences* of Peter Lombard and delivering eleven "relections." These were two-hour lectures on a subject of their choice that chairs of theology were obliged to give once a year on pain of a fine.

It was the Spanish emperor's desire that Vitoria would be his envoy to the Council of Trent. As Vitoria's frail health made that impossible,

---

[6] Vicente Beltrán de Heredia, *Domingo de Soto: Estudio biográfico documentado* (Salamanca: Cultura Hispánica, 1961).

[7] Beltrán de Heredia, *Soto*, 64.

Soto was asked to go in his stead, along with Bartolomé de Carranza, later Bishop of Toledo and Primate of the Church in Spain (on whom more below) in 1545.[8] At Trent and its aftermath, Soto forcefully reacted against what he saw as signs of Lutheranism.[9] He confronted the General of the Servites, Agostino Bonuccio, on the matter of justification.[10] He also confronted the Dominican Ambrosio Catarino on the question of whether one can have certitude of faith of being in the state of grace.[11] It is hard not to see Soto, contrary to Beltrán de Heredia's assessment, as displaying an overzealous attitude during the council. For example, according to the imperial ambassador Diego Hurtado de Mendoza, Soto called Spanish theologian Francisco Herrera a "heretic" in public.[12] Soto's general attitude seems to have been out of step in a council held in a spirit of relative open-mindedness.[13]

---

[8] On Soto in Trent, see Beltrán de Heredia, *Soto*, 118–73; also Stephen Gaetano, "*Fides quae per charitatem operatur*: A Study and Translation of Domingo de Soto's *De natura et gratia*" (PhD diss., University of Notre Dame, 2015).

[9] Wim Decock has noted the fundamentally anti-Lutheran character of the scholarly efforts of theologians such as Domingo de Soto, particularly in their biblical exegesis. Decock, "Law and the Bible in Spanish Scholasticism," in *The Oxford Encyclopedia of the Bible and Law*, ed. Brent A. Strawn, vol. 2 (New York: Oxford University Press, 2015), 326–27.

[10] Beltrán de Heredia, *Soto*, 149–54. See also Robert E. McNally, "Freedom and Suspicion at Trent: Bonuccio and Soto," *Theological Studies* 29 (1968): 752–62.

[11] Beltrán de Heredia, *Soto*, 175–205. See also Jesús Olazarán, "La controversia 'Soto-Catarino-Vega' sobre la certeza de la gracia," *Estudios eclesiásticos* 61 (1942): 145–84; and Alister E. McGrath, *Iustitia Dei: A History of the Christian Doctrine of Justification*, 3rd ed. (Cambridge: Cambridge University Press, 2005), 337.

[12] Beltrán de Heredia, *Soto*, 155; Constancio Gutiérrez, *Españoles en Trento* (Valladolid: Instituto "Jerónimo Zurita," 1951), 408–9.

[13] For a recent reassessment of the Council of Trent, see John W. O'Malley, "What Happened and Did Not Happen at the Council of Trent," and Günther Wassilowsky, "The Myths of the Council of Trent and the Construction of

In parallel with Trent, tensions between Charles V and Pope Paul III over Piacenza in Italy, which had been seized by the emperor, increased. Pope Paul's strategy was to delay his support of imperial proposals for religious accommodation in Germany until Piacenza was restored to him.[14] After Pedro de Soto, the emperor's confessor, asked for license to leave, Domingo de Soto was asked in 1548 to step in, and he moved to the imperial court in Augsburg in February. Cardinal Nicolas Perrenot de Granvelle, Charles's chancellor, hoped that Domingo would be more sympathetic to his political designs than Pedro had been.[15]

Initially Soto seemed to meet Granvelle's expectations, for example by defending the imperial territorial pretensions over Piacenza.[16] However, Soto resigned the post after only a year and a half. He never said why, but according to Diego Hurtado de Mendoza, Soto objected to the emperor's exchequer policies. These objections, according to Hurtado, included how the king favored the wealthier foreign and Spanish merchants over poor Spanish merchants, created unnecessary offices simply for the purpose of selling them indiscriminately, collected more revenue by selling lands given in *encomienda* (a form of trust) to military orders (before which these lands were rented for the benefit of the church),[17] and introduced new ordinances and laws with the mere purpose of selling monopolies—for example, the general prohibition against producing playing cards allegedly introduced to sell

---

Catholic Confessional Culture," both in *The Council of Trent: Reform and Controversy in Europe and Beyond*, ed. Wim François and Violet Soen, vol. 1 (Göttingen: Vandenhoeck & Ruprecht, 2018), 49–68 and 69–98.

14 Beltrán de Heredia, *Soto*, 221–30.

15 Beltrán de Heredia, *Soto*, 217.

16 Beltrán de Heredia, *Soto*, 221.

17 See Francisco Fernández Izquierdo, *La Orden Militar de Calatrava en el siglo XVI* (Madrid: CSIC, 1992), 60–61.

Introduction

exceptional permits. In short, the cash-strapped emperor kept using increasingly morally dubious ways of collecting revenue.[18]

Soto was one of the four theologians asked to participate in a junta convened on the event of Juan Ginés de Sepúlveda's *Democrates secundus*.[19] This Latin dialogue was written at the behest of Spanish colonists against new laws in the West Indies in 1542. These laws aimed at restraining the ill treatment of Native Americans by the colonists. The University of Salamanca blocked the publication of *Democrates secundus*. So the emperor convened in Valladolid a commission of theologians and jurists and members of the *Consejo Real de Indias* to discuss one of the matters raised by the dialogue, namely, whether the Native Americans could be fought against by reason of their infidelity. Soto wrote the summary of the arguments presented by Sepúlveda in one session and those of his fellow Dominican Bartolomé de las Casas, the prolix defender of the Native Americans, in five sessions, as well as their respective responses to each other. For the final meeting, only Carranza and Soto, from among the initial four theologians, attended. We know that one of them abstained from voting against Sepúlveda. Beltrán de Heredia has argued—against Marcel Bataillon—that this was not Soto.[20]

Returning to Salamanca in 1552, Soto was given the Chair of Prima (the morning lecture) by acclamation, that is, without having to compete. Soto was held in such high esteem that he was even allowed, at his request, to teach the prestigious morning lecture in the afternoon so he was able to use the morning for writing.[21]

---

[18] Beltrán de Heredia, *Soto*, 233, from the chronicler Florián de Ocampo found in the manuscript *Noticias de varios sucesos acaecidos, desde el año de 1521 hasta el 1558, copiadas de un códice copiado de mano*, 2 vols., Biblioteca Nacional de España, MSS 9936–9937.

[19] Juan Ginés de Sepúlveda, *Democrates segundo*, vol. 3 of *Obras completas*, ed. Coroleu Lletget (Pozoblanco: Ayuntamiento de Pozoblanco, 1997), 39–134.

[20] Beltrán de Heredia, *Soto*, 269–70; Marcel Bataillon, "Pour l' 'Epistolario' de Las Casas. Une lettre et un brouillon," *Bulletin hispanique* 56 (1954): 373–74.

[21] Beltrán de Heredia, *Soto*, 305.

A later sad episode in Soto's life concerns the inquisitorial process against his friend Bartolomé Carranza de Miranda. Carranza was prosecuted for a *Commentary of the Catechism* that the Holy Office suspected of Lutheranism. In his biography of Soto, Beltrán de Heredia aims to clear Soto's name of allegations made by earlier historians that he showed himself a duplicitous and disloyal friend in the matter of Carranza.[22]

The agreed-on facts are that Carranza privately asked Soto to read his *Commentary* and point out anything that could be seen as unorthodox, which Soto did, noting sixty-two propositions that required amending or correcting, even though they were not "formally erroneous."[23] Roughly at the same time, the end of 1558, Soto was asked by the Inquisition to go to Valladolid, where a number of suspected Lutherans had recently been burned in an *auto da fe*. Soto was to theologically assess (*calificar*) Carranza's book along with fellow Dominicans Melchor Cano (a personal enemy of Carranza) and Domingo de Cuevas. Initially Soto thought he could avoid going to Valladolid and could reassure the Inquisition of Carranza's orthodoxy by accepting the Inquisition's request to see his comments on the book that he had sent to Carranza.[24] However, seeing these comments only made the Inquisition more eager. Soto reported to Carranza that he did not wish to take part in this examination nor to get a reputation as a "prosecutor of works or spiritual persons," and that he was not pleased with the way he was treated by the Inquisition. However, Carranza urged Soto to go to Valladolid in the hope that a benign assessment by someone with the status of Soto would help his case. This step backfired. In Valladolid, Soto was requested to judge the propositions of the book with the utmost possible rigor and was prevented from leaving town until he produced a censure.[25] According to Melchor Cano, Soto was

---

[22] Juan Antonio Llorente, *Historia crítica de la inquisición de España*, vol. 3 (Barcelona: Oliva, 1835), 217–20.

[23] Beltrán de Heredia, *Soto*, 466.

[24] Beltrán de Heredia, *Soto*, 466–67.

[25] Beltrán de Heredia, *Soto*, 478.

also threatened by some of Carranza's supporters that if he was too rigorous, he should be prepared to have his own writings rigorously scrutinized and denounced should anything dubious be found.[26] Soto produced two censures, each of a different set of propositions and submitted to the Holy Office on January 12, 1559.[27] The fact that he censured Carranza even though he was known to be his friend provided ammunition for the Inquisition to continue the process, which finally ended in 1574 with an ambiguously injurious sentence by Pope Gregory XIII after the process had been relocated to Rome.[28]

It is clear that Soto was placed in a very difficult position given the intimidating way in which Valdez, the Inquisitor General, conducted the procedure. A charitable account would hold that Soto tried but failed to appease the Inquisition without worsening the situation of Carranza, and that given the atmosphere of fear, no more could be reasonably asked from him. However, as Tellechea Idígoras, an expert on Carranza concludes, Soto's conduct toward his friend left much to be desired.[29]

Afflicted by gout, Soto breathed his last on November 15, 1560 in the presence of fellow Dominican theologian Domingo Báñez. His body was buried in the chapter chapel of San Esteban, now called "The Theologians' Pantheon."

Works and Major Contributions

Domingo de Soto's works include a *Summula* of logic for use in the course of arts; a commentary on Aristotle's *Dialectics*, which included separate commentaries on Porphyry's *Isagoge*, the *Categories*, *Peri Hermeneias*, *Topics*, *Prior and Posterior Analytics*, and *Sophistici Elen-*

---

[26] Beltrán de Heredia, *Soto*, 477.

[27] Beltrán de Heredia, *Soto*, 485, 490.

[28] See José Ignazio Tellechea Idígoras, "El final de un proceso: Sentencia original de Gregorio XIII y abjuración del Arzobispo Carranza," *Scriptorium victoriense* 23 (1976): 202–32.

[29] José Ignacio Tellechea Idígoras, *El Arzobispo Carranza y su tiempo*, vol. 2 (Madrid: Guadarrama, 1968), 300.

chi;³⁰ a commentary on Aristotle's *Physics*; and a companion volume, *Questions on the Eight Books of the Physics*.³¹

Only after Trent did Soto devote himself systematically to theology and morality. From this period came *On Nature and Grace* in 1547.³² His longest and most important work, the *Ten Books on Justice and Right*, was originally published in 1553, and a substantially revised version was published in 1556–1557.³³ Soto's two-volume *Commentary on*

---

30 This is Aristotle's *Organon* with the addition of Porphyry's introduction to the *Categories*.

31 These are the first early editions of Soto's works: *Summulae* (Burgos: Juan de la Junta, 1529); *In Dialecticam Aristotelis: Isagoge Porhyrii in Aristotelis Categoria; de Demonstratione* (Salamanca: Juan de la Junta, 1543); *Super octo libros Physicorum commentaria* (Salamanca: Juan de la Junta, [1545]); *Super octo libros Physicorum Quaestiones* (Salamanca: Juan de la Junta, [1545]); *De justitia et jure, libri decem* (Salamanca: Andrés de Portonariis, 1553); *Commentarium in Quartum Sententiarum* (Salamanca: Juan de Cánova, 1557); *De natura et gratia* (Venice: Juntas, 1547); *Epistolam divi Pauli ad Romanos commentarii* (Antwerp: Joannis Steels, 1550); *De cavendo juramentorum abusu* (Salamanca: Andrés de Portonariis, 1552); *Suma de la doctrina Cristiana* (Salamanca: Andrés de Portonariis, 1552); *Annotationes in commentarios Joannis Feri Moguntinensis super Evangelium Joannis* (Salamanca: Andrés de Portonariis, 1554); *De extremo judicio* (n.p., 1545); *Tratado del amor de Dios* (Madrid: Blas Roman, n.d.). For a full list of first publications, published manuscripts, and the location of unpublished manuscripts, see María del Pilar Cuesta Domingo, *Estudio Crítico: Domingo de Soto* (Madrid: Fundacion Ignacion Larramendi, 2013), http://www.larramendi.es/esc_sal/i18n/consulta/registro.do?id=9757; idem, *Domingo de Soto y su Obra* (Segovia: Colegio Universitario de Segovia, 1996); and idem, "La obra literaria de Soto, *Qui scit Sotum scit totum*," in *Domingo de Soto en su mundo*, ed. Mariano Cuesta Domingo (Segovia: Colegio Universitario "Domingo de Soto," 2008), 239–90.

32 Stephen Gaetano has translated the text of this work into English and included it in his doctoral dissertation, "*Fides quae per charitatem operatur*."

33 This modified version includes a new and separate book on oaths. See Wim Decock, "Soto, *On Justice and Right*," in *The Formation and Transmission of Western Legal Culture: 150 Books that Made the Law in the Age of Printing*, ed. Serge Dauchy et al. (Cham: Springer, 2016), 94–96.

Peter Lombard's Sentences saw the light in 1557 and 1560 respectively. Other published works include nine of his relections; the summary of the Valladolid controversy; a treatise on the love of God; a commentary on Paul's Letter to the Romans; a sermon on the final judgment delivered at Trent; a commentary critical of the *Commentary on John* by Johann Wild (latinized Ferus), a Franciscan preacher from Mainz; a fragment on the question of just war in the context of the Americas; and a *Summa* of Christian doctrine.

Given the volume of Soto's writings, it is hard to describe in detail his contributions. However, we can point to contributions that have attracted the most scholarly interest—leaving aside for now the question of the poor, which is examined in greater detail below.

Some historians of science have taken an interest in Soto possibly preceding Galileo in positing that bodies fall at a uniform rate of acceleration.[34] Concerning Soto's theology, the focus has been on his analysis of scriptural exegesis, heresy, and the sacraments.[35] Scholars interested in Soto's legal and political thought have brought attention to his theories of human liberty, subjective rights, and *dominium*;

---

[34] The most complete compilation of secondary bibliography on Soto, as well as other Salamanca authors, can be found in Miguel Anxo Pena González, *Aproximación bibliográfica a la(s) "Escuela(s) de Salamanca"* (Salamanca: Universidad de Salamanca, 2008). On Soto's dynamics, see William A. Wallace, *Domingo de Soto and the Early Galileo: Essays on Intellectual History* (London: Routledge, 2018). On Soto's logic, see Saverio Di Liso, *Domingo de Soto: dalla logica alla scienza* (Bari: Levante, 2000); Vicente Muñoz Delgado, "Domingo de Soto y la ordenación de la enseñanza de la lógica," *Ciencia Tomista* 87 (1960): 467–528; and idem, *Lógica formal y filosofía en Domingo de Soto (1494–1560)* (Madrid: Monasterio de Poyo, 1964).

[35] Indicative texts on Soto as theologian include Juan de Belda Plans, "Domingo de Soto (1495–1560) y la reforma de la teología en el siglo XVI," *Anales valentinos* 42 (1995): 193–221; idem, "Domingo de Soto y la defensa de la teología escolástica en Trento," *Scripta teológica* 27 (1995): 423–58. See also Dionisio Borobio García, *El sacramento de la penitencia en la Escuela de Salamanca: Francisco de Vitoria, Melchor Cano y Domingo de Soto* (Salamanca: Universidad Pontificia, 2006).

his views on limited government; and his take on the *ius gentium*.[36] Those interested in morality have discussed Soto's views on certainty and moral doubt, the moral right to privacy, and the status of reputation.[37] Concerning Soto's work on the ethics of economic exchanges, scholars have discussed his views on the just price, on the morality of commercial enterprise, and on usury.[38] Soto's views on the question

---

[36] Indicative works include Venancio Diego Carro, *Domingo de Soto y su doctrina jurídica* (Madrid: Minuesa, 1943); Jaime Brufau Prats, *El pensamiento político de Soto y su concepción del poder* (Salamanca: Universidad de Salamanca, 1960); Domingo Ramos-Lissón, *La ley según D. Soto (estudio Teológico jurídico)* (Pamplona: Universidad de Navarra, 1976); Karl J. Becker, *Die Rechtfertigungslehre nach Domingo de Soto: Das Denken eines Konzilsteilnehmers vor, in und nach Trient* (Rome: Gregorian University, 1964); Jörg Tellkamp, "Esclavitud, dominio y libertad humana según Domingo de Soto," *Revista española de filosofía medieval* 11 (2004): 129–37; Paula Oliveira e Silva, "The Concept of *ius gentium*: Some Aspects of Its Doctrinal Development from the 'School of Salamanca' to the Universities of Coimbra and Évora," in *The Concept of Law (lex) in the Moral and Political Thought of the "School of Salamanca,"* ed. Kirstin Bunge et al. (Leiden: Brill, 2016), 106–125; and Franco Todescan, "*Jus gentium medium est intra jus naturale et jus civile*: la 'double face' du Droit des Gens dans la scolastique espagnole du 16ème siècle," in *The Roots of International Law: Liber amicorum Peter Haggenmacher*, ed. Pierre-Marie Dupuy and Vincent Chetail (Leiden: Brill, 2013), 138–43.

[37] See Andreas Blank, "Domingo de Soto on Justice for the Poor," *Intellectual History Review* 25 (2015): 136–46; Francisco O'Reilly, *Duda y opinión: La conciencia moral en Soto y Medina* (Pamplona: Universidad de Navarra, 2006); and Daniel Schwartz, *The Political Morality of the Late Scholastics: Civic Life, War and Conscience* (Cambridge: Cambridge University Press, 2019), 58–77. For broader studies on the question of moral doubt in late scholasticism, see Rudolf Schuessler, *The Debate on Probable Opinions in the Scholastic Tradition* (Leiden: Brill, 2019); and Stefania Tutino, *Shadows of Doubt: Language and Truth in Post-Reformation Catholic Culture* (Oxford: Oxford University Press, 2014).

[38] Indicative works include José Barrientos García, *Un siglo de moral económica en Salamanca (1526–1629): Francisco de Vitoria y Domingo de Soto* (Salamanca: Universidad de Salamanca, 1995); André Azevedo Alves and

of the possible grounds for the conquest of America and the right treatment of Native Americans has also attracted scholarly interest.[39]

I will briefly comment on one of Soto's most original views: that natural law and rights extend to nonhuman animals.[40] His view features in two contexts: the question whether natural law comprises one or more precepts and the distinction between natural law and the *ius gentium*.[41] On the question of the many precepts of natural law, Soto starts by arguing that natural law consists of precepts that are naturally known, corresponding to or identical with natural inclinations. The human natural inclinations divide into those founded in the mere fact of our existence, in the fact of our being animals, and in the fact of our being rational animals. It follows, according to Soto, that nonhuman animals are in a way also governed by natural law since they have

---

José Manuel Moreira, "Virtue and Commerce in Domingo de Soto's Thought: Commercial Practices, Character, and the Common Good," *Journal of Business Ethics* 113 (2013): 627–38; Horacio Rodríguez Penelas, "Contribución de Domingo de Soto a la gestación del pensamiento económico hispanoamericano," in *La ley natural como fundamento moral y jurídico en Domingo de Soto*, ed. Juan Cruz (Pamplona: EUNSA, 2007), 223–40; Juan Velarde Fuertes, "Domingo de Soto y la economía," in *Domingo de Soto en su mundo*, ed. Mariano Cuesta Domingo (Segovia: Colegio Universitario "Domingo de Soto," 2008), 43–58; and Jose María Garrán Martínez, "Pobreza y usura en el pensamiento ético y jurídico de Domingo de Soto" (PhD thesis, Universidad de Valladolid, 1991).

[39] See Vicente Beltrán de Heredia, "El maestro Domingo de Soto en la controversia de las Casas con Sepúlveda," *Ciencia Tomista* 45 (1932): 35–49, 177–93; Paulino Castañeda Delgado, "La ética colonial en Domingo de Soto," in *Domingo de Soto en su mundo*, ed. Mariano Cuesta Domingo (Segovia: Colegio Universitario "Domingo de Soto," 2008), 73–90.

[40] As suggested to me by Wim Decock, Conrad Summenhart may have been one of Soto's influences in attributing rights to animals. See Jussi Varkemaa, "Can Animals Have Rights? Conrad Summenhart and Francisco de Vitoria at the Margins of Rights Language," in *Rights at the Margins: Historical, Legal and Philosophical Perspectives*, ed. Virpi Mäkinen et al. (Leiden: Brill, 2020), 153–70.

[41] Soto, *Iustitia et iure*, 1.4.2 (p. 31); 3.1.3 (p. 196), respectively.

natural inclinations (or precepts), such as preserving themselves in being and procreating.[42]

When Soto comes to the question of distinguishing the *ius naturale* from the *ius gentium*, he first distinguishes between the conformity of *ius naturale* to nature "absolutely considered" on the one hand and nature "in order to a certain end and according to circumstances" on the other. As examples of conformity with nature "absolutely considered," Soto mentions the fact that men and women are suited for procreation and the father's care for feeding the offspring. He believed that nonhuman animals apprehend nature in this first sense by instinct. So in a way "natural right in the simple sense of the term (*ius cum simpliciter est naturale*) such as the society between male and female and the nurturing of the offspring is common to all animals."[43] What nonhuman animals lack and we have is, for Soto, the capacity to adapt the right to the consecution of ends according to circumstance. Soto gives the example of property. Absolutely considered, nature does not indicate the need of property. However, given our human psychological postlapsarian propensities to laziness and greediness, private property will contribute to a more efficient use of the land than keeping it common. So our goals (efficiency in resource use) and our circumstances (our postlapsarian laziness) make it the case that reason indicates the need for private property. Property as a natural right is not common to all animals but only to humans.

Soto's commentators are divided on the merit of his conceptions of natural law and rights. Bernice Hamilton argues that Soto was confused about natural law.[44] Annabel Brett, by contrast, sees Soto as having a "coherent response ... to the basic problem of how to reconcile the traditional distinction between natural and free agency, embedded in

---

[42] Soto, *Iustitia et iure*, 1.4.2 (p. 31); 3.1.3 (p. 196).

[43] Soto, *Iustitia et iure*, 3.1.3 (p. 196).

[44] Bernice Hamilton, *Political Thought in Sixteenth-Century Spain: A Study of the Political Ideas of Vitoria, De Soto, Suárez and Molina* (Oxford: Oxford University Press, 1963), 8.

the scholastic account of salvation and meritorious action, with the naturalistic ethics and politics of Aristotle."[45]

Soto's way of distinguishing between the natural law and the *ius gentium* was objected to by some late scholastic authors such as Fray Luis de León and Bartolomé Medina.[46] According to Soto, natural law in its proper sense includes only those principles naturally and innately known to us, whereas the *ius gentium* includes those conclusions arrived at by processes of reasoning on the basis of the former.[47] Critics charge that Soto's view absurdly places the commandments of the Decalogue, which are not innately or naturally known to us, within the *ius gentium*. For example, "do not steal" presupposes cognizance of the institution of property, an institution the need of which cannot be appreciated without reasoning.[48]

Historical and Polemical Context of the *Deliberation*

Sixteenth-century Europe was marked by an acceleration of the pace of rural migration to the urban centers, mostly in the wake of bad harvests. Across Protestant and Catholic Europe, cities reformed their poor laws to make it more difficult for the outside poor to use their streets and churches to beg for alms.[49]

---

[45] Annabel S. Brett, *Liberty, Right and Nature: Individual Rights in Late Scholastic Thought* (Cambridge: Cambridge University Press, 1997), 137.

[46] Fray Luis de León, *Tratado sobre la Ley*, ed. José Barrientos García and Emiliano Fernández Vallina (El Escorial: Escurialenses, 2005), 226–27; Bartolomé de Medina, *Expositio in primam secundae* (Venice: Petrum Mariam Bertanum, 1602), q. 94, a. 4. See Oliveira e Silva, "Concept of *ius gentium*," 113; Todescan, "*Jus gentium medium*," 138–43.

[47] Soto, *Iustitia et iure*, 1.5.4 (p. 44).

[48] Soto addresses this objection in *Iustitia et iure*, 1.5.4 (p. 45).

[49] On the poverty debate, see Linda Martz, *Poverty and Welfare in Habsburg Spain* (Cambridge: Cambridge University Press, 1983); Félix Santolaria Sierra, "Estudio introductorio," in *El gran debate sobre los pobres en el siglo XVI: Domingo de Soto y Juan de Robles 1545*, ed. Félix Santolaria Sierra (Barcelona: Ariel, 2003), 11–46; María Jiménez Salas, *Historia de la Asistencia Social en*

Many of the beggars in Spain came from northern countries. Miguel de Cervantes illustrates this, as well as the widespread suspicion that many beggars faked their poverty, when he writes about Sancho Panza being approached by German beggars. Sancho offers them bread and cheese, but the beggars demand money instead. It turns out that these beggars in fact have plenty of food and money.[50]

The best known of the new poor policies and a model for the rest were the ordinances of Ypres of 1525, upheld by the Sorbonne theologians in 1531[51] and famously defended by Juan Luis Vives in *De subventione pauperum* (1526), addressed to the government of Bruges.[52]

Spain was by no means alien to such proposals. With growing insistence, requests to outlaw street begging and expel foreign beggars were made from 1518 onwards.[53] In 1523, the Cortes (representative assemblies usually summoned by the king) of Valladolid reiterated previous requests from 1518 to deny access to the poor from outside the cities. In 1521, the city of Córdoba ordered foreign beggars to be expelled.[54] In 1525, the Cortes of Toledo requested an examination of each purported poor person, after which only those found to be genuinely poor would be eligible for a license to beg.[55] Soto tells us that in the Cortes of Madrid of 1528 and 1534 there were new requests

---

España en la Edad Moderna (Madrid: CSIC, 1958); Michel Cavillac, "Estudio introductorio," in Cristóbal Pérez de Herrera, *Amparo de pobres*, ed. Michel Cavillac (Madrid: Espasa-Calpe, 1975), i–xxiv; and Ole Peter Grell et al., eds., *Health Care and Poor Relief in Counter-Reformation Europe* (London: Routledge, 1999).

[50] Miguel de Cervantes Saavedra, *Don Quijote de la Mancha*, pt. 2, ch. 54.

[51] J. Nolf, *La réforme de la bienfaisance publique à Ypres au XVIe siècle* (Ghent: Van Goethem, 1915), 119–20.

[52] Juan Luis Vives, *De subventione pauperum sive de humanis necessitatibus, libri II*, ed. Constant Matheeussen et al., vol. 4 of *Selected Works of Juan Luis Vives*, ed. Charles Fantazzi (Leiden: Brill, 2002).

[53] Martz, *Poverty and Welfare*, 14.

[54] Martz, *Poverty and Welfare*, 14.

[55] Santolaria Sierra, "Estudio introductorio," 20.

Introduction

to tackle the problem of the poor. It was not until 1540, however, after a severe drought the previous year, that a new poor law was legislated for all of Castile.

The law established that the genuinely poor could only beg within their hometown after being issued a license that had to be renewed annually. The license was issued only after the recipient had made confession and taken communion. Beggars were not to take with them their children who were older than five years so that these children could work or learn trades. Begging in churches and monasteries at time of mass was prohibited. Blind persons, mendicant friars, and students could beg in their hometowns if equipped with the right licenses. Begging outside one's birthplace was allowed only in time of epidemic or some other emergency. Pilgrims, including foreign ones, could beg along the Way of Santiago so long as they did not deviate from the way.[56]

The command to enforce this law appeared with the text of the law in 1540, which was signed by the members of the royal council, and the law was followed by an "Instruction" establishing its precise form of execution.[57] So he would not be seen as arguing against a law that was already in force, Soto claims that the law had not in fact come into effect at the time he wrote his essay. He argues on the unconvincing ground that the "Instruction" specifying the practicalities of enforcement appears *after* the signatures of the members of the royal council and is followed by only the signature of Francisco del Castillo, the Chambers' Notary (*escribano de cámara*).[58]

---

[56] *Quaderno de algunas leyes, que no estan en el libro de las pragmaticas, que por mandado de sus Magestades se Mandan imprimir este año de 1540* (Salamanca: Juan de Canova, 16 November 1540).

[57] *Quaderno*. The law in question is titled in the index as "Que los pobres pidan en sus tierras y no en otras partes, y la orden que en ellos se ha de tener." After the signatures of the members of the council, it reads: "Instruction [*sic*] de la orden que se ha de tener en el cumplimiento y execucion de las leyes que hablan sobre los pobres."

[58] Beltrán de Heredia, *Soto*, 244.

Circumstances and Precedents

The literature on poverty preceding Soto's *Deliberation* is in two main genres. One genre is nonacademic polemical tracts urging for the introduction of the reforms. Some works have a more critical tone toward the policy proposals, such as Gabriel del Toro's *Tesoro de la Misericordia* (1536).[59] The second genre is moral theology. The most important of these works are *Codex de eleemosyna*, by the Alcalá theologian Juan de Medina,[60] and Alfonso de Castro's *De potestate legis poenalis*.[61]

According to Soto, before the introduction of new poor laws, the city of Zamora consulted the theologians of Salamanca on the new laws word by word. There were some objections. The final document was then sent from Zamora, and Soto was assured by the unnamed person who provided the document that his objections had been taken on board.[62] He signed his approval, as did the other Salamanca theologians consulted, "almost without exception," as noted by Robles.[63]

Soto says he was very surprised when in a conversation with Cardinal Tavera—the driving force behind the reforms—after Soto had raised objections to the new poor laws, the cardinal showed him the document Soto himself had signed approving those very laws. Given

---

[59] Gabriel del Toro, *Tesoro de la misericordia divina y humana* (Valencia: Pedro de Huete, 1575, first ed. 1536). Most of the early literature supporting the introduction of the new laws came from Flanders. See Schwartz, *Political Morality*, 62.

[60] Juan de Medina lived from 1490 to 1546. This Juan de Medina should not to be confused with the later critic of Soto, Juan Robles (1492–1572), who sometimes went by "Juan de Medina."

[61] Juan de Medina, *Codex de eleemosyna* (Alcalá: Athanasio Salzedo, 1544), fol. 173v; Alfonso de Castro, *De potestate legis poenalis libri duo* (Louvain: Antonii Maria Bergagne, 1557), bk. 1, fol. 231.

[62] See below, pp. 14–15.

[63] "Casi sin faltar ninguno," as noted by Juan de Robles in *De la orden que en algunos pueblos de España se ha puesto en la limosna, para remedio de los verdaderos pobres*, in *El gran debate*, 159.

the deceptive misrepresentation of his views and the potential harm to his integrity, Soto set out to set the record straight by writing the *Deliberation.*

Soto's account, notes Linda Martz, is not entirely credible. Is it really plausible, she asks, to believe that Soto did not read the Zamora statutes, which were no longer than a few pages, before signing them?[64] Soto's conduct brings to mind his portrayal by Diego Hurtado de Mendoza as "obstinate and furious, very resolute in his opinion, but then less constant than he should be if these [his opinions] are not brought to his attention."[65]

Soto had been personally involved in poverty relief before. In 1540, when almost no wheat was left in Salamanca, he was commissioned by the university to bring from Toledo the wheat promised by Cardinal Tavera. Later that year, Soto was asked to consider ways of dealing with a plague of locusts.[66] It is not clear exactly what his job was as there were dedicated judges (*jueces de langosta*) in charge of enforcing the methods of extermination.[67] Soto was also one of the two university representatives chosen to join three *regidores* in 1544 to "examine the poor of Salamanca." One of the main jobs of the deputies was to prevent door-to-door begging.[68] This means that Soto helped to enforce some of the new poor laws to which he would posteriorly object. Later, in 1557–1559, when excessive rains brought back hunger to Salamanca, Soto and Melchor Cano made a register of the poor to be helped by the Convent of San Esteban and set up a kitchen for the poor.

The *Deliberación en la causa de los pobres* was published simultaneously in Latin and Spanish on January 30, 1545.[69] There are very minor

---

[64] Martz, *Poverty and Welfare*, 23.

[65] Beltrán de Heredia, *Soto*, 233.

[66] Beltrán de Heredia, *Soto*, 81.

[67] Jerónimo Castillo de la Bovadilla, *Politica para corregidores* (Madrid: Imprenta de la Gazeta, 1755), vol. 2, bk. 5, ch. 4, n. 41 (p. 682).

[68] Beltrán de Heredia, *Soto*, 90. The source of the citation in the minutes of the *claustro* (university council) of Salamanca is not provided.

[69] Both versions have been included in Brufau Prats, ed., *In causa pauperum deliberatio*, in Soto, *Relecciones y opúsculos*, II-2. Beltrán de Heredia says

differences, though some of them revealing, between the Latin and Spanish versions.⁷⁰ The Spanish version is less solemn, often leaning toward a colloquial tone.

The Latin edition translated here was published in Venice in 1547. Venetian proposals to reform poor law along the lines of Ypres's legislation began in earnest around 1527 with comprehensive legislation passed in 1529. However, this law was not systematically enforced until 1545. Soto resided in Venice for a few months during 1546, away from Trent, while attending to the printing of his *De natura et gratia*. This explains the timing of the Venetian senate's request to make his essay newly available. Soto promises in the introduction a more careful, less rushed version of the original text. Although in the end there are fewer changes than the reader is led to expect, the Venetian edition differs from the *princeps editio* in that, importantly, it contains a direct commentary on Juan Luis Vives's defense of the poor law reforms in his *De subventione pauperum*.⁷¹

The essay was written, as Soto himself tells us, in only twelve days, first in Latin and then translated by Soto into Spanish. It is often pointed out that Soto was able to write the essay quickly because he based it on his unpublished relection or lecture on almsgiving (*eleemosyna*) given in the academic year 1542–1543, the manuscript of which has been lost.⁷² Soto had also discussed almsgiving before when he lectured on Aquinas's *Summa theologiae*, IIa-IIae, q. 32, in the weeks following

---

that the book was published in Latin in January and in Spanish in March; however, the two first printings of each version bear the same date. Beltrán de Heredia, *Soto*, 89.

⁷⁰ One revealing difference is that in the Spanish version, the largest community of duty mentioned is that made up of all Christians, whereas in the Latin version, it is the whole human community. See below, p. 34; Schwartz, *Political Morality*, 73.

⁷¹ On Soto's Venetian sojourn, see Beltrán de Heredia, *Soto*, 166. On the Venetian poor law reforms, see Brian Pullan, *Rich and Poor in Renaissance Venice: The Social Institutions of a Catholic State, to 1620* (Oxford: Blackwell, 1971), 239–327, esp. 297.

⁷² As reported by Melchor Cano, cited in Beltrán de Heredia, *Soto*, 89.

Introduction

Christmas 1539. A possible autograph of these lectures has been preserved as a manuscript in the Vatican (Ott. lat. 782 ff. 112r–115v) and has been transcribed by Antonio J. Garín.[73] In those lectures, Soto discusses questions on almsgiving that were commonly discussed by earlier theologians. In these lectures, however, Soto considers only the interpersonal duties of almsgiving and includes nothing on institutional arrangements, let alone the new poor reforms.

The same is true of a manuscript at the Biblioteca Nacional de México that has been considered for decades by many Soto scholars to be the notes of a student who attended Soto's 1536–1539 lectures. This manuscript covers commentary on Aquinas's articles on almsgiving that is missing from the Vatican manuscript. However, upon direct inspection of this manuscript, it appears highly doubtful that it bears direct or indirect relationship to Soto.[74] Be that as it may, when the

---

[73] Antonio J. Garín, *El precepto de la limosna en un comentario inédito del Maestro Fray Domingo de Soto sobre la cuestión 32 de la II-II de Santo Tomás: Fragmento de la disertación para el doctorado en la Facultad de Teología en la Pontificia Universidad Gregoriana* (Santiago de Chile: Pontificia Universitas Gregoriana, 1949). The date of the lectures is given on p. 60. Also in Karl Deuringer, *Probleme der Caritas in der Schule von Salamanca* (Freiburg: Herder, 1959). According to Jericó Bermejo, the Vatican Ott. lat. 782 consists of the notes made by Soto, corrected by him and his secretary (presumably Diego de Chaves).

[74] Karl Josef Becker, Vicente Beltrán Heredia, and Ignacio Jericó Bermejo, among others, have considered the Mexican manuscript to consist of expanded lecture notes of Soto's teaching at Salamanca from 1536 to 1539. Becker defends this attribution to Soto in Becker, "La tradición manuscrita de las prelecciones de Domingo de Soto," *Archivo teológico Granadino* 29 (1966): 163, 168. It seems that these authors did not physically see the manuscript for decades and worked from a microfilm since the manuscript they refer to as MS. 940 was recatalogued as MS. 614 in 1950. The attribution of the MS to Soto should be doubted for various reasons. First, the MS contains many more questions and articles from *Summa theologiae*, IIa-IIae, than those that appear in the Vatican manuscript. Second, Soto's questions and articles that do feature in both manuscripts are much more expansively discussed in the Mexican MS than in the Vatican one. These differences cannot really be put

author of this manuscript addresses the question of whether, when giving alms, we ought to prefer those closer to us over strangers, he defends the priority of giving help to those more proximate to us.

Given that Aquinas's text on almsgiving provided a perfect occasion for Soto to discuss the poor reforms, an occasion that he failed to

---

down to the Mexican MS being a student's explanation of the lecture. Third, the Mexican MS contains a note in handwriting that is different than the handwriting of the main writer, reporting that the manuscript contains the "estudios de Fray Juan Vicente." This is probably a Dominican Salamanca theologian born in 1544 in Astorga, Spain, who was at some point at San Esteban and died in 1596. Vicente was born after Soto gave his lectures. Fourth, in the third folio, the same hand notes that the MS was left by a Juan de Salas to the library of the Franciscan Convent of Vetoxla (Huetoxla), and the volume has indeed the mark of the fire of Vetoxla. Juan de Salas, born in Villa Porcuna, Andalusia, was a Definitor of the Holy Office and chosen Provincial of the Franciscan Santo Evangelio Province of Mexico in 1605. The estimated life spans of Salas and Vicente overlap.

Jericó Bermejo ventures that the MS may have been written by a *Julio Salas*. Bermejo, "Domingo de Soto o.p., Repasos solemnes y lecciones ordinarias. Textos manuscritos sobre la Sagrada Escritura (1536–1539). Primera parte," *Archivo teológico Granadino* 81 (2008): 305. I have not been able to confirm the historical existence of this person. The only piece of evidence connecting the Mexican MS to Soto is that in the top of the first folio we read "$\overset{\circ}{2}.\overset{\circ}{2}$ S Tho. a magistro Soto incipit." The current catalogue information of the MS is as follows:

    Classification: MS MS.614
    Local Classification: MS.614
    Author: Vicente, Juan
    Title: Materia theologica [manuscrito]: quaestiones de Fise [sic.], Spe et Charitate, de Eleemosyna, de paterna correctione, de vitiis et virtutibus in particulari.
    Description: [i, 212] h.; 22 cm.
    System Number: 000045014

I would like to thank Lic. Alberto Octavio Partida Gómez, the Director of the Fondo Reservado of the Biblioteca Nacional de México, for the effort he invested in tracking down this manuscript and also Prof. Armando Pavón Romero, Dr. Marco Toste, and Prof. Wim Decock for their further assistance.

take advantage of, we must conclude that it is likely that Soto devoted careful thinking to the new policies only after 1540.

Critical Responses

Soto's *Deliberation* was met with a response from the Benedictine Juan de Robles (also known as Juan de Medina) in his *On the Ordinances Adopted by Some Towns of Spain for the Remedy of the True Poor*, published only two months after Soto's essay. Robles attempts to refute Soto point by point. He suggests that some of the opposition to the reforms comes from people who are worried that it will become known how little they give to charity, since under the new system alms would be given by subscription to a common fund so that the town government would know the exact amount contributed by each person.[75]

Other notable contributions to this debate in Spain, again in favor of the reforms and proposing practical measures, are Juan Bernal Díaz de Luco's *Doctrina y amonestación caritativa* (1547),[76] Miguel de Giginta's *Tratado de remedio de pobres* (1579),[77] and Cristóbal Pérez de Herrera's *Amparo de los pobres* (1598).[78]

Scholastic theologians, save for some exceptions (Alfonso de Castro, Martín de Ledesma, Gabriel Vázquez, and later Pedro de Lorca, Eloy de la Bassée, and Antonino Diana), failed to engage Soto.[79] While

---

[75] Beltrán de Heredia, *Soto*, 88; the source in Robles is not provided.

[76] "La 'doctrina y amonestación charitativa' (1547) de Juan Bernal Diaz de Luco. Transcripción y aproximación a su contexto social," in *Historia y teoría de la educación. Estudios en honor del profesor Emilio Redondo García*, ed. Javier Laspalas Pérez (Pamplona: EUNSA, 1999), 311–28. Luco was present at the Council of Trent.

[77] Miguel Giginta, *Tratado del remedio de los pobres*, ed. Félix Santolaria Sierra (Barcelona: Ariel, 2000).

[78] Cristóbal Pérez de Herrera, *Amparo de pobres*, ed. Michel Cavillac (Madrid: Espasa-Calpe, 1975).

[79] Martín de Ledesma, *Secunda quartae* (Coimbra: Juan Alvarez, 1560), q. 15, a. 7, fols. 128b–31a; Alfonso de Castro, *De potestate legis poenalis*, bk. 1, fols. 23r-v; Gabriel Vázquez, *De eleemosyna*, in idem, *Opuscula moralia* (Alcalá:

Introduction

Soto found some defenders and some critics, overall his *Deliberation* failed to ignite a lasting debate.

Synopsis

Soto's essay contains twelve chapters. After the dedicatory opening in chapter 1, Soto surveys in chapter 2 the policy developments and his personal involvement leading up to the writing of the essay. Chapter 3 describes the ills of vagrancy and the ways of eradicating it. Chapters 4 and 5 argue against closing the city to the outside poor. Chapter 6 argues against imposing new restrictions on the freedom of movement and defends the pilgrims' right to collect alms along the Way of Santiago. Chapter 7 questions the purity of the motivations behind the proposed poor law reforms. Chapter 8 explains the moral precept of almsgiving. Chapter 9 chastises the newly introduced ways of examining the poor. Chapter 10 questions the appropriateness of conditioning benefits on the moral and religious improvement of the poor. Chapters 11 and 12 argue against the prohibition on door-to-door begging and the forced seclusion of the poor in dedicated institutions.

Main Thesis

Soto considers three measures proposed by the laws to be particularly problematic from a moral point of view: (1) the exclusion of foreign beggars from the city, (2) the subjection of poor people to humiliating and counterproductive examinations, and (3) the prohibition of door-to-door begging.

The reasons given against these measures are both normative and related to efficiency. On the efficiency front, Soto doubts that the new measures will in fact improve the situation of the poor or collect more alms. Some of the arguments to this effect are based on the peculiarities

---

Juan Gracián, 1617), ch. 3, dub. 2 (p. 24); Pedro de Lorca, *Commentaria et disputationes in secundam secundae* (Madrid: Luis Sánchez, 1614), sect. 3, d. 37, a. 9, n. 19 (p. 822); Eloy de la Bassée, *Flores totius theologiae practicae* (Lyon: Anisson, 1657), p. 270, n. 8; Antoninus Diana, *Resolutiones morales* (Venice: Franciscus Baba, 1653), res. 36 (p. 131).

of the character of Spaniards at the time. One such peculiarity was their low level of compliance with law. Soto notes, "Compared to other people, the Spaniards are more easily persuaded by hearing a personal plea and seeing the misery of the beggars than by being coerced by law."[80] What worked in other places did not necessarily work in Spain, because in other places "people are more inclined toward the common good and are more easily bound by law than we are."[81] There was some truth in what Soto noted, at least if judging from the candid acknowledgment of Robles, the defender of the reforms, on the paucity of the alms collected through the subscription system.[82]

A second peculiar trait of Spaniards at the time, according to Soto, was their sense of honor.[83] He points out "men would rather suffer from extreme hunger than to have their mendicancy publicly revealed, which is certainly true of the Spanish, who consider honor more valuable than life." The consequence was that the planned examination of those poor called *envergonzantes* ended up defeating its purpose. These were people from affluent classes who fell into poverty but, fearing social dishonor, maintained appearances to the extent possible and thus did not beg. Soto tells us how sometimes horsemen and officers afoot went by the street to register the poor, causing great shame.[84] Registering these poor people was bound to be counterproductive because it likely led many of them to refrain from asking for help so they would not fall into disrepute.

Both Spanish attitudes, according to Soto, predicted the failure of the new system. Other arguments from efficiency include his skepticism about the eagerness of waged state officials to obtain alms. Waged officials will invest less effort in securing alms compared to the poor whose lives depend on it. In addition, mercy is to a large extent

---

[80] See below, p. 105.

[81] My translation. Cf. below, p. 106.

[82] Martz, *Poverty and Welfare*, 22; Robles, *De la orden*, in *El gran debate*, 105.

[83] See below, p. 88.

[84] See below, p. 88.

awakened by the sight of the suffering of the poor as opposed to the sight of a well-dressed state official.[85]

On the normative level, Soto appeals to a number of grounds. Concerning the exclusion of the foreign poor, he emphasizes the natural rights and *ius gentium* rights that everyone has, including the poor, native and foreign.[86] These include the right to use public space; the right not to be punished in the absence of crime, and where there is one, not to be disproportionately punished; and the right of everyone to try to secure a livelihood, a right which involves not only the right to self-preservation but also the right to secure nonvital needs.[87] Soto also insists on the duties of hospitality.[88] He argues that geographic regions that are unequally endowed within the realm should help each other, as should the different social classes, just as a body has functionally different organs that are interdependent and mutually supportive.[89]

According to Soto, the new provisions also violate the *ius commune*, namely, the common legal system that developed in continental Europe from the eleventh century onward. They do so by conflicting with a Roman imperial constitution prescribing that foreigners with the status of freemen who are incapable of working because of old age or sickness must be allowed to remain in the city.[90]

One of the sources of Soto's moral discomfort was the fact that the new reforms shine the moral spotlight on just one section of the population. The poor will now be subject to a moral and legal surveillance from which the wealthy are exempted. Help to the poor will no longer be meant simply to alleviate poverty but rather will become a tool of

---

[85] See below, p. 107.

[86] See Schwartz, *Political Morality*, 64–67.

[87] See below, pp. 30–34.

[88] See below, pp. 35–37. See Annabel S. Brett, *Changes of State: Nature and the Limits of the City in Early Modern Natural Law* (Princeton, NJ: Princeton University Press: 2011), 19–20.

[89] See below, pp. 32–34. On Soto's use of the body metaphor, see Schwartz, *Political Morality*, 71–74.

[90] A transcription of the *Authenticum* can be found in Soto, *Relecciones y opúsculos*, II-2, 368–70; and Brufau Prats, *El pensamiento político*, 367–70.

moral reform. In effect, a citizen's freedom from public scrutiny and censure will be made dependent on economic power.[91]

Soto states, "For there are those in the republic who, by means of less licit contracts and even fraud and deceit, secretly steal the property of others and to a far greater degree than the vagabonds. But none of these machinations are aimed at them."[92] Soto goes on, "For surely, if the poor had the opportunity, perhaps they would be able to discover many faults in us which they could correct."[93] Later he adds, "For how many workmen or public servants are there in the republic who by fraud steal many more possessions than that entire crowd of able-bodied beggars...? Yet men are able to tolerate their fraud and robberies with an even mind. But there is no way to convince those same men to tolerate a false pauper who is depriving someone of a miserable little coin by means of clever tricks, namely, by dragging his nudity, trembling, hunger, and infirmity around with him."[94]

Soto also identifies some of the less obvious problems of replacing door-to-door begging with centralized alms collection. Centralized collection and dispersion of basic help will, according to Soto, provide equally basic help to every poor person. Yet needs, including nutritional ones, can vary drastically from one individual to another. Moreover, centralized welfare will occasionally deny the poor the gift of not just bread or fruit but "a delicacy which God and nature granted to the human race."[95] This denial may seem a minor consideration, but it is telling of a more general worry: centralized welfare for Soto brings about a standardization of help that is blind to the individuality of poor people. To say that a poor person is as capable as a wealthy person of appreciating a glass of good wine or a good cake is to say that he or she is equally endowed with individual aesthetic preferences and

---

[91] See below, pp. 54–57, 67–91.

[92] See below, p. 56.

[93] See below, pp. 56–57.

[94] See below, pp. 74–75.

[95] See below, p. 100. Here I use "delicacy" (*manjar*) as in the Spanish version, rather than simply "food" (*cibus*) as in the Latin, because it seems to better convey Soto's point.

capacity for refined choice. The poor are not just bread eaters; they are capable of appreciating, no less than the rich, the good things in life.

Wim Decock, citing Diana Wood, has observed that Soto's view is "rooted in a static worldview centered around the idea that the rich and poor were 'bound together in a symbiotic relationship of mutual necessity.'"[96] Following the Greek fathers such as John Chrysostom, whom he cited often in the *Deliberation*, Soto may have thought that the poor are spiritually necessary because their existence allows the faithful to exercise charity and provides them with an example of humility. Awareness of the pervasiveness of this patristic and medieval worldview also suggests that in rejecting the reforms, Soto may have worried that the proposed centralized poor relief constituted a usurpation of the traditional role of the church as the divinely designated caretaker of the poor. Certainly other attackers of the new reforms, such as Lorenzo de Villavicencio, were motivated by this worry. These motivations may have fueled Soto's attack against the poor relief reforms.

It is no doubt important to understand Soto's approach to the poor within the general medieval mindset. However, such contextualization of his ideas should not blind us to the force of an important question pressed by Soto's *Deliberation*. This question concerns the nature of the love that we owe to the poor. Does love for the poor mean turning them into non-poor, or does it mean loving them *as poor people*? Soto does not celebrate or romanticize poverty, and he is not against getting people out of poverty, even though he is pessimistic about the chances of success. However, he believed that Christian charity is mainly expressed in our love of our neighbor as he or she now is—a poor person—and not only as what he or she could be.

---

[96] Wim Decock, "Social Crisis and the Rule of Law," *Rivista internazionale di diritto commune* 28 (2017): 159, citing Diana Wood, *Medieval Economic Thought* (Cambridge: Cambridge University Press, 2002), 42–43.

Literature

Primary Sources

Bassée, Eloy de la. *Flores totius theologiae practicae.* Lyon: Anisson, 1657.

Castillo de la Bovadilla, Jerónimo. *Politica para corregidores.* Madrid: Imprenta de la Gazeta, 1755.

Castro, Alfonso de. *De potestate legis poenalis libri duo.* Louvain: Antonii Maria Bergagne, 1557.

Diana, Antoninus. *Resolutiones morales.* Venice: Franciscus Baba, 1653.

Diaz de Luco, Juan Bernal. "La 'doctrina y amonestación charitativa' (1547) de Juan Bernal Diaz de Luco. Transcripción y aproximación a su contexto social." Edited by Félix Santolaria Sierra. In *Historia y teoría de la educación. Estudios en honor del profesor Emilio Redondo García*, edited by Javier Laspalas Pérez, 311–28. Pamplona: EUNSA, 1999.

Giginta, Miguel. *Tratado del remedio de los pobres.* Edited by Félix Santolaria Sierra. Barcelona: Ariel, 2000.

Ledesma, Martín de. *Secunda quartae.* Coimbra: Juan Alvarez, 1560.

León, Fray Luis de. *Tratado sobre la Ley.* Edited by José Barrientos García and Emiliano Fernández Vallina. El Escorial: Escurialenses, 2005.

Lorca, Pedro de. *Commentaria et disputationes in secundam secundae.* Madrid: Luis Sánchez, 1614.

Medina, Bartolomé de. *Expositio in primam secundae.* Venice: Petrum Mariam Bertanum, 1602.

Medina, Juan de. *Codex de eleemosyna.* Alcalá: Athanasio Salzedo, 1544.

Ocampo, Florian de. *Noticias de varios sucesos acaecidos, desde el año de 1521 hasta el 1558, copiadas de un códice copiado de mano.* 2 vols. Biblioteca Nacional de España, MSS 9936–9937. http://bdh.bne.es/bnesearch/detalle/bdh0000050832.

Pérez de Herrera, Cristóbal. *Amparo de pobres.* Edited by Michel Cavillac. Madrid: Espasa-Calpe, 1975.

Quaderno de algunas leyes, que no estan en el libro de las pragmaticas, que por mandado de sus Magestades se Mandan imprimir este año de 1540. Salamanca: Juan de Canova, 16 November 1540.

Schöll, Rudolf, and Wilhelm Kroll, eds. *Corpus Iuris Civilis: Novellae*. Berlin: Wiedmann, 1912.

Sepúlveda, Juan Ginés de. *Democrates segundo*. Vol. 3 of Juan Ginés de Sepúlveda, *Obras completas*, edited by Coroleu Lletget. Pozoblanco: Ayuntamiento de Pozoblanco, 1997.

Soto, Domingo de. *Annotationes in commentarios Joannis Feri Moguntinensis super Evangelium Joannis*. Salamanca: Andrés de Portonariis, 1554.

———. *Commentarium in Quartum Sententiarum*. Salamanca: Juan de Cánova, 1557.

———. *De cavendo juramentorum abusu*. Salamanca: Andrés de Portonariis, 1552.

———. *De extremo judicio*. n.p., 1545.

———. *De iustitia et iure libri decem*. Edited by Venancio Diego Carro and P. Marcelino González Ordóñez. 5 vols. Madrid: Instituto de Estudios Políticos, 1968.

———. *De justitia et jure, libri decem*. Salamanca: Andrés de Portonariis, 1553.

———. *De natura et gratia*. Venice: Juntas, 1547.

———. *Epistolam divi Pauli ad Romanos commentarii*. Antwerp: Joannis Steels, 1550.

———. *In causa pauperum deliberatio*. Edited by Jaime Brufau Prats. In Domingo de Soto, *Relecciones y opúsculos*, II-2, edited by Sixto Sánchez-Lauro and Jaime Brufau Prats, 187–361. Salamanca: San Esteban, 2011.

———. *In Dialecticam Aristotelis: Isagoge Porhyrii in Aristotelis Categoria; de Demonstratione*. Salamanca: Juan de la Junta, 1543.

———. *Suma de la doctrina Cristiana*. Salamanca: Andrés de Portonariis, 1552.

———. *Summulae*. Burgos: Juan de la Junta, 1529.

———. *Super octo libros Physicorum commentaria*. Salamanca: Juan de la Junta, [1545].

———. *Super octo libros Physicorum Quaestiones*. Salamanca: Juan de la Junta, [1545].

———. *Tratado del amor de Dios*. Madrid: Blas Roman, n.d.

Soto, Domingo de, and Juan de Robles. *El gran debate sobre los pobres en el siglo XVI: Domingo de Soto y Juan de Robles 1545*. Edited by Félix Santolaria Sierra. Barcelona: Ariel, 2003.

Toro, Gabriel del. *Tesoro de la misericordia divina y humana*. 1536. Valencia: Pedro de Huete, 1575.

Vázquez, Gabriel. *De eleemosyna*. In Gabriel Vázquez, *Opuscula moralia*, 1–59. Alcalá: Juan Gracián, 1617.

Vicente, Juan. "Materia theologica [manuscrito]: quaestiones de Fise [sic.], Spe et Charitate, de Eleemosyna, de paterna correctione, de vitiis et virtutibus in particulari." N.d. MS 614, 000045014. Biblioteca Nacional de México.

Villavicencio, Lorenzo de. *Oeconomia sacra circa pauperum curam*. Antwerp: Christophorus Plantini, 1564.

Vives, Juan Luis. *De subventione pauperum sive de humanis necessitatibus, libri II*. Edited by Constant Matheeussen, Charles Fantazzi, and Jeanine De Landtsheer. Vol. 4 of *Selected Works of Juan Luis Vives*, edited by Charles Fantazzi. Leiden: Brill, 2002.

Secondary Sources

Azevedo Alves, André, and José Manuel Moreira. "Virtue and Commerce in Domingo de Soto's Thought: Commercial Practices, Character, and the Common Good." *Journal of Business Ethics* 113 (2013): 627–38.

Barrientos García, José. *Un siglo de moral económica en Salamanca (1526–1629): Francisco de Vitoria y Domingo de Soto*. Salamanca: Universidad de Salamanca, 1995.

Bataillon, Marcel. "Pour l' 'Epistolario' de Las Casas. Une lettre et un brouillon." *Bulletin hispanique* 56 (1954): 366–87.

Becker, Karl Josef. *Die Rechtfertigungslehre nach Domingo de Soto: Das Denken eines Konzilsteilnehmers vor, in und nach Trient*. Rome: Gregorian University, 1964.

———. "La tradición manuscrita de las prelecciones de Domingo de Soto." *Archivo teológico Granadino* 29 (1966): 125–80.

Belda Plans, Juan de. "Domingo de Soto (1495–1560) y la reforma de la teología en el siglo XVI." *Anales valentinos* 42 (1995): 193–221.

———. "Domingo de Soto: y la defensa de la teología escolástica en Trento." *Scripta teológica* 27 (1995): 423–58.

Beltrán de Heredia, Vicente. "El maestro Domingo de Soto en la controversia de las Casas con Sepúlveda." *Ciencia Tomista* 45 (1932): 35–49, 177–93.

———. *Domingo de Soto: Estudio biográfico documentado*. Salamanca: Cultura Hispánica, 1961.

Bermejo, Jericó. "Domingo de Soto o.p., Repasos solemnes y lecciones ordinarias. Textos manuscritos sobre la Sagrada Escritura (1536–1539). Primera parte." *Archivo teológico Granadino* 81 (2008): 293–495.

Blank, Andreas. "Domingo de Soto on Justice for the Poor." *Intellectual History Review* 25 (2015): 133–46.

Borobio García, Dionisio. *El sacramento de la penitencia en la Escuela de Salamanca: Francisco de Vitoria, Melchor Cano y Domingo de Soto*. Salamanca: Universidad Pontificia, 2006.

Brett, Annabel S. *Changes of State: Nature and the Limits of the City in Early Modern Natural Law*. Princeton, NJ: Princeton University Press: 2011.

———. *Liberty, Right and Nature: Individual Rights in Late Scholastic Thought*. Cambridge: Cambridge University Press, 1997.

Brufau Prats, Jaime. *El pensamiento político de Soto y su concepción del poder*. Salamanca: Universidad de Salamanca, 1960.

Castañeda Delgado, Paulino. "La ética colonial en Domingo de Soto." In *Domingo de Soto en su mundo*, edited by Mariano Cuesta Domingo, 73–90. Segovia: Colegio Universitario "Domingo de Soto," 2008.

Cuesta Domingo, María del Pilar. *Domingo de Soto y su Obra*. Segovia: Colegio Universitario de Segovia, 1996.

———. *Estudio Crítico: Domingo de Soto*. Madrid: Fundacion Ignacion Larramendi, 2013. http://www.larramendi.es/esc_sal/i18n/consulta/registro.do?id=9757.

———. "La obra literaria de Soto, *Qui scit Sotum scit totum*." In *Domingo de Soto en su mundo*, edited by Mariano Cuesta Domingo, 239–90. Segovia: Colegio Universitario "Domingo de Soto," 2008.

Decock, Wim. "Law and the Bible in Spanish Scholasticism." In *The Oxford Encyclopedia of the Bible and Law*, edited by Brent A. Strawn, vol. 2, 325–31. New York: Oxford University Press, 2015.

———. "Social Crisis and the Rule of Law." *Rivista internazionale di diritto commune* 28 (2017): 159–78.

———. "Soto, *On Justice and Right*." In *The Formation and Transmission of Western Legal Culture: 150 Books that Made the Law in the Age of Printing*, edited by Serge Dauchy, Georges Martyn, Anthony Musson, Heikki Pihlajamäki, and Alain Wijffels, 94–96. Cham: Springer, 2016.

Deuringer, Karl. *Probleme der Caritas in der Schule von Salamanca*. Freiburg: Herder, 1959.

Diego Carro, Venancio. *Domingo de Soto y su doctrina jurídica*. Madrid: Minuesa, 1943.

Di Liso, Saverio. *Domingo de Soto: dalla logica alla scienza*. Bari: Levante, 2000.

Fernández Izquierdo, Francisco. *La Orden Militar de Calatrava en el siglo XVI*. Madrid: CSIC, 1992.

Gaetano, Stephen. "*Fides quae per charitatem operatur*: A Study and Translation of Domingo de Soto's *De natura et gratia*." PhD diss., University of Notre Dame, 2015.

Garín, Antonio J. *El precepto de la limosna en un comentario inédito del Maestro Fray Domingo de Soto sobre la cuestión 32 de la II-II de Santo Tomás: Fragmento de la disertación para el doctorado en la Facultad de Teología en la Pontificia Universidad Gregoriana*. Santiago de Chile: Pontificia Universitas Gregoriana, 1949.

Garrán Martínez, Jose María. "Pobreza y usura en el pensamiento ético y jurídico de Domingo de Soto." PhD thesis, Universidad de Valladolid, 1991.

Grell, Ole Peter, Andrew Cunningham, and Jon Arrizabalaga, eds., *Health Care and Poor Relief in Counter-Reformation Europe*. London: Routledge, 1999.

Gutiérrez, Constancio. *Españoles en Trento*. Valladolid: Instituto "Jerónimo Zurita," 1951.

Hamilton, Bernice. *Political Thought in Sixteenth-Century Spain: A Study of the Political Ideas of Vitoria, De Soto, Suárez and Molina*. Oxford: Oxford University Press, 1963.

Jiménez Salas, María. *Historia de la Asistencia Social en España en la Edad Moderna*. Madrid: CSIC, 1958.

Llorente, Juan Antonio. *Historia crítica de la inquisición de España*. Vol. 3. Barcelona: Oliva, 1835.

Martz, Linda. *Poverty and Welfare in Habsburg Spain*. Cambridge: Cambridge University Press, 1983.

McGrath, Alister E. *Iustitia Dei: A History of the Christian Doctrine of Justification*. 3rd ed. Cambridge: Cambridge University Press, 2005.

McNally, Robert E. "Freedom and Suspicion at Trent: Bonuccio and Soto." *Theological Studies* 29 (1968): 752–62.

Muñoz Delgado, Vicente. "Domingo de Soto y la ordenación de la enseñanza de la lógica." *Ciencia Tomista* 87 (1960): 467–528.

———. *Lógica formal y filosofía en Domingo de Soto (1494–1560)*. Madrid: Monasterio de Poyo, 1964.

Nolf, J. *La réforme de la bienfaisance publique à Ypres au XVIe siècle*. Ghent: Van Goethem, 1915.

Olazarán, Jesús. "La controversia 'Soto-Catarino-Vega' sobre la certeza de la gracia." *Estudios eclesiásticos* 61 (1942): 145–84

Oliveira e Silva, Paula. "The Concept of *ius gentium*: Some Aspects of Its Doctrinal Development from the 'School of Salamanca' to the Universities of Coimbra and Évora." In *The Concept of Law (lex) in the Moral and Political Thought of the "School of Salamanca,"* edited by Kirstin Bunge, Marko J. Fuchs, Danaë Simmermacher, and Anselm Spindler, 106–125. Leiden: Brill, 2016.

O'Malley, John W. "What Happened and Did Not Happen at the Council of Trent." In *The Council of Trent: Reform and Controversy in Europe and Beyond*, edited by Wim François and Violet Soen, vol. 1, 49–68. Göttingen: Vandenhoeck & Ruprecht, 2018.

O'Reilly, Francisco. *Duda y opinión: La conciencia moral en Soto y Medina*. Pamplona: Universidad de Navarra, 2006.

Pena González, Miguel Anxo. *Aproximación bibliográfica a la(s) "Escuela(s) de Salamanca."* Salamanca: Universidad de Salamanca, 2008.

Pullan, Brian. *Rich and Poor in Renaissance Venice: The Social Institutions of a Catholic State, to 1620.* Oxford: Blackwell, 1971.

Ramos-Lissón, Domingo. *La ley según D. Soto (estudio teológico jurídico).* Pamplona: Universidad de Navarra, 1976.

Rodríguez Penelas, Horacio. "Contribución de Domingo de Soto a la gestación del pensamiento económico hispanoamericano." In *La ley natural como fundamento moral y jurídico en Domingo de Soto,* edited by Juan Cruz, 223–40. Pamplona: EUNSA, 2007.

Schuessler, Rudolf. *The Debate on Probable Opinions in the Scholastic Tradition.* Leiden: Brill, 2019.

Schwartz, Daniel. *The Political Morality of the Late Scholastics: Civic Life, War and Conscience.* Cambridge: Cambridge University Press, 2019.

Tellechea Idígoras, José Ignacio. "Domingo de Soto y Bartolomé Carranza." *Hispania sacra* 13 (1960): 423–42.

———. *El Arzobispo Carranza y su tiempo.* Vol. 2. Madrid: Guadarrama, 1968.

———. "El final de un proceso: Sentencia original de Gregorio XIII y abjuración del Arzobispo Carranza." *Scriptorium victoriense* 23 (1976): 202–32.

Tellkamp, Jörg. "Esclavitud, dominio y libertad humana según Domingo de Soto." *Revista española de filosofía medieval* 11 (2004): 129–37.

Todescan, Franco. "*Jus gentium medium est intra jus naturale et jus civile*: la 'double face' du Droit des Gens dans la scolastique espagnole du 16ème siècle." In *The Roots of International Law: Liber amicorum Peter Haggenmacher,* edited by Pierre-Marie Dupuy and Vincent Chetail, 121–80. Leiden: Brill, 2013.

Tutino, Stefania. *Shadows of Doubt: Language and Truth in Post-Reformation Catholic Culture.* Oxford: Oxford University Press, 2014.

Varkemaa, Jussi. "Can Animals Have Rights? Conrad Summenhart and Francisco de Vitoria at the Margins of Rights Language." In *Rights at the Margins: Historical, Legal and Philosophical Perspectives,* edited by Virpi Mäkinen, Jonathan Robinson, Pamela Slotte, and Heikki Haara, 153–70. Leiden: Brill, 2020.

Velarde Fuertes, Juan. "Domingo de Soto y la economía." In *Domingo de Soto en su mundo*, edited by Mariano Cuesta Domingo, 43–58. Segovia: Colegio Universitario "Domingo de Soto," 2008.

Wallace, William A. *Domingo de Soto and the Early Galileo: Essays on Intellectual History*. London: Routledge, 2018.

Wassilowsky, Günther. "The Myths of the Council of Trent and the Construction of Catholic Confessional Culture." In *The Council of Trent: Reform and Controversy in Europe and Beyond*, edited by Wim François and Violet Soen, vol. 1, 69–98. Göttingen: Vandenhoeck & Ruprecht, 2018.

Wood, Diana. *Medieval Economic Thought*. Cambridge: Cambridge University Press, 2002.

Translators' Note

The *Deliberation on the Cause of the Poor* was originally published in 1545 in both Latin and Spanish.[1] This English translation starts from a 1547 Venetian reprint of the original Latin text, to which Soto had given his full assent and support. The text of this reprint, our source text, is freely available on the website of the Bavarian State Library in Munich.[2]

Soto originally published his *Deliberation* in two languages in order to spread his point of view beyond the borders of Spain, which we learn from his preface to the work. Thus the Latin version of the publication reached the city of Venice and stirred heated debate there. During Soto's

---

[1] The Latin version was entitled *Ad maximum atque adeo clarissimum Hispaniarum principem dominum Philippum, invictissimi Caesaris Caroli V primogenitum Fratris Dominici Soto Segobiensis … in causa pauperum deliberatio* (Salamanca: Juan de Junta, 1545). The Spanish version was entitled *Al muy alto y muy poderoso señor el Principe de España don Philippe primogenito del invictissimo Cesar don Carlos quinto deliberacion en la causa de los pobres del maestro fray Domingo de Soto …* (Salamanca: Juan de Junta, 1545).

[2] *Fratris dominici Soto Segobiensis, Ordinis Praedicatorum, In causa pauperum deliberatio. Cum privilegio Venetorum senatus* (Venice: unknown printer, 1547), http://mdz-nbn-resolving.de/urn:nbn:de:bvb:12-bsb10173442-5. Slight variations exist between this and other versions of the 1547 Venice edition, especially in chapter 12, as can be learned by comparing it with another edition available on the website of the Bavarian State Library, http://mdz-nbn-resolving.de/urn:nbn:de:bvb:12-bsb11283074-6.

stay in the city between 1545 and 1547, the Senate of Venice invited him to publish a new edition. Soto states that this new edition would respond to arguments raised after 1545 by opponents of his viewpoint. However, Soto claims to have found no arguments against his point of view which had not already been refuted in his older publication. Nevertheless, he was still willing to edit and improve the work, which allegedly he had written in no more than twelve days. In addition to a new preface, Soto included a short digression on Venice's role as a harbor for pilgrims to the Holy Land and a refutation of arguments raised by his opponent Juan Luis Vives.

Our translation keeps as close as possible to the original Latin text. However, at times preserving readability required us to make adaptations in the sentence structure and the style. Soto's detailed references to works of other authors were moved from the main text and the margins to the footnotes. Most of the time, these references had to be expanded and adapted to modern standards. Tacit references in the Latin original were, to the best of our ability, made explicit in the footnotes. Such additional references are preceded by "Ed. note" to indicate that they are not mentioned in the original text but are the result of our analysis. In deciphering both explicit and implicit references, we greatly benefited from the modern edition of Soto's *Deliberation* by Jaime Brufau Prats and Sixto Sánchez-Lauro.[3] We also drew inspiration from an annotated French translation, based on the Spanish version of the *Deliberation*, by Edouard Fernández-Bollo.[4] However, we have not always followed their interpretations and editorial choices.

When Soto cited Spanish legislation, we added references to the relevant sections of the *Nueva* and *Novísima Recopilación*: more complete references and a reprint of a number of legal sources used by Soto can be found in the edition by Brufau Prats and Sánchez-Lauro. Soto's frequent quotations of the Vulgate Bible were translated directly from

---

[3] Domingo de Soto, *In causa pauperum deliberatio*, ed. Jaime Brufau Prats, in Soto, *Relecciones y opúsculos*, II-2 (Salamanca: San Esteban, 2011).

[4] Domingo de Soto, *La cause des pauvres*, trans. Edouard Fernandez-Bollo (Paris: Dalloz, 2013).

Latin into English, although we did make use of the Douai-Rheims and King James Bibles as sources of inspiration. In Soto's original text, references to the Bible only include chapter numbers. So we have added verse numbers in accordance with modern practice, but using the Vulgate's verse numbers rather than those of modern English editions. All other citations of ancient works, including lengthy quotations from the work of Chrysostom, were also directly translated from Latin into English.

Quite often, the Latin terminology is of a rather technical nature or peculiar in other ways. In these cases, the English translation is accompanied by a footnote mentioning the original Latin term. Effort has been made to translate the most important of such terms consistently, including *egeni* as "the needy," *pauperes* as "the poor," *mendici* as "beggars," *peregrini* as "pilgrims," and *vagabundi* as "vagabonds."

We would like to thank Prof. Dr. Wim Decock for his suggestion to translate the *Deliberation*, his continuous assistance during our work, and his great insight. On a personal note, Joost would like to express his gratitude to his fiancée, Benedict, for her support, interest, and enthusiasm. Meanwhile, Jeremiah would like to thank his amazing wife, Tina, for her unwavering support and encouragement in this endeavor. This translation would not have been possible without them.

— Joost Possemiers and Jeremiah Lasquety-Reyes

Abbreviations

Cod.	Corpus Iuris Civilis, Codex
Dig.	Corpus Iuris Civilis, Digesta
Inst.	Corpus Iuris Civilis, Institutiones
Nov.	Corpus Iuris Civilis, Novellae
Dec. Grat.	Corpus Iuris Canonici, Decretum Gratiani
Dec. Greg.	Corpus Iuris Canonici, Decretales Gregorii IX
Clem.	Constitutiones Clementinae
PG	*Patrologiae cursus completus: Series graeca.* Edited by J.-P. Migne. 162 vols. Paris, 1857–1886.
PL	*Patrologiae cursus completus: Series latina.* Edited by J.-P. Migne. 217 vols. Paris, 1844–1864.

Deliberation on the Cause of the Poor

To the Reader

Domingo de Soto of Segovia
Friar of the Order of Preachers

When I was compelled to depart from the Council of Trent to go to Venice for business, a number of noble patricians, full of mercy in their hearts, conveyed to me that the cause of the beggars was being contested there.[1] Previously, I had written a deliberation on that cause for the Most Serene Prince of Spain.[2] They told me that the booklet—which had already reached Venice—was of great support to them in their attempts to secure the evangelical liberty of the *legitimate* poor; for who could bear imposters and sycophants pretending to be poor? They added, however, that there were also people expressing the opposite opinion, and that I would render a great service, first and foremost to God, but also to the Most Illustrious and Wisest Senate of Venice, if I would take it upon myself to reply to their objections. Who would not have willingly undertaken such a cause? So I began perusing the relevant writings, even of authors who had, before us, expressed a different view. However, even though I had not previously taken any of these works into consideration, I was still not able to find any point

---

[1] Ed. note: For Soto, beggars are not only people who roam the streets and ask for alms, but also those who receive assistance and stay at home; cf. ch. 12, p. 116.

[2] Ed. note: The "Most Serene Prince of Spain" is Prince Philip II of Spain, son of Emperor Charles V.

of objection in them, which I had not—at least in my view—already responded to as well as I could. Nevertheless, considering that I had, at the time, pondered the issue for only twelve days, I decided to think it through a second time and make my responses even more in accordance with God's will and more useful to this Most Renowned Republic.

The sacred prudence of that Most Excellent Prince and of the Senators of the Republic is certainly demonstrated by their willingness to hear anyone's opinions on a matter so strongly commended by Christ, the Father of the Poor, as they intend to carry out the policy most in line with the gospel. There was otherwise no need to change the form of this little work, which had already been dedicated to the Most Serene Prince, especially since the laws which are now being considered for adoption in the Most Illustrious Dominion[3] are more or less identical to the ones introduced before in Spain.

---

[3] Ed. note: i.e., Venice.

1

Dedicatory Epistle

Deliberation on the Cause of the Poor

by Domingo de Soto of Segovia,
Friar of the Order of Preachers

To the Greatest and Most Renowned Prince of Spain, Lord Philip, Firstborn of the Most Invincible Emperor Charles V

No reason could ever have prompted me, Greatest Prince, to write this letter to Your Magnitude, had I not often read in many authors how much humanity a prince should possess and how much clemency is owed by your noble lineage of heroic princes to listen to men of every class and condition. Equally important is that I have heard from many people how much humanity and clemency you have personally demonstrated, as befitting your house and paternal ancestry. Considering that you have done so in matters of lesser importance, we can now assume, not only that you would be open to listen with humanity to the views of many experts, but that you would even request their counsel. Naturally, once Your Highness, who sits on the throne of the emperor, will have rendered judgment in this affair, nothing will be left for your subjects but to listen to your decision and obey your commands.

I am fully aware of how little authority I have to add anything of importance to either side of the debate, which remains so controversial. Also, in giving my opinion, I am not seeking to change anything that has already been laid down by rule. Rather, I would be satisfied if all possible inconveniences entailed by the rules already laid down are examined carefully, thereby allowing these rules to be carried out more cautiously, more prudently, and more in accordance with God's will. On that basis, the interests of the miserable and poor will be provided for in a better way. One can therefore render no service more agreeable to Your Imperial Majesty and Dignity, or more beneficial to the Republic. For Christ, our Savior, not only wanted, preached, and admonished us to take care of the poor, but also ordered us to do so, making very powerful promises and threats.

Four years ago,[1] some cities,[2] certainly not the least within the Spanish domain of our emperor, started to separate poor people from vagabonds, impose order on them, and collect and distribute alms following a predetermined rationale and method. The objective was to prevent the beggars from going door to door, so that the poor might be spared this labor and the rich might be free from their brutal insistence. Furthermore, alms should not be handed out blindly. Rather, a selection ought to be made to separate the able-bodied[3] from the larger group and to make sure that those who are truly in need receive more copious alms.

Undoubtedly, nobody can be found who does not consider this new plan a magnificent one, the product of a Christian mind and worthy of praise, favor, and zeal from everyone to the best of their

---

[1] Ed. note: i.e., ca. 1541, since the reference "*his retro quattuor annis*" can already be found in the original Salamanca edition of 1545. Domingo de Soto, *In causa pauperum deliberatio*, ed. Jaime Brufau Prats, in Soto, *Relecciones y opúsculos*, II-2 (Salamanca: San Esteban, 2011), 206.

[2] Ed. note: A case in point is the city of Toledo, which implemented a welfare reform in 1541 after the model of Zamora's poor laws of 1540; see L. Martz, *Poverty and Welfare in Habsburg Spain: The Example of Toledo* (Cambridge: Cambridge University Press, 1983). For an overview of initiatives in other Castilian cities, see J. Arrizabalaga, "Poor Relief in Counter-Reformation Castile: An Overview," in *Health Care and Poor Relief in Counter-Reformation Europe*, ed. O. P. Grell, A. Cunningham, and J. Arrizabalaga (London: Routledge, 1999), 151–76.

[3] Ed. note: According to Soto, the able bodied are "those who are not only in good health but also strong enough to work and yet feign and simulate infirmity to beg and wander around the world" (ch. 3, p. 24).

ability. However, since the topic carries so much weight, we should not be surprised if all people cannot easily find agreement on it. No work immediately merits to be called virtuous on the basis of its subject matter alone, as honorable as it might be, for our goal, which is virtuousness, is not attained spontaneously. Each work has to be "clothed" with many additional qualities which cannot be discovered and clearly perceived if the opinions of many other people are not taken into account. It frequently occurs that the most wise and well-informed men are able to foresee great risks on the basis of simple doubts expressed by ignorant people like us. For "a wise man will hear" (as the proverb of Solomon says), "and he will be wiser."[4] Therefore neither you, Most Noble Prince, nor anyone else should ascribe any of my words to a personal desire to oppose anyone or to an appetite for contention.

I do not claim such great ability in any affair, nor could I have moved forward without incurring blame in this one, had I had that attitude. Therefore, there is no reason for anyone to stop me and start quarreling. As I have announced at the beginning, the thrust of my plea—if it should have any strength at all—is only to make sure that the laws governing the poor are laid down with the greatest possible circumspection. In this way, standing alongside truly great men who on a daily basis contribute the most generous alms to this affair, I will donate two brass mites in accordance with my own insignificance, just like the poor widow in the Gospel.[5]

After all, the alms that we debtors owe to the destitute do not consist of bread alone. Indeed, let me refer to the words of Gregory:

> If someone possesses much insight, he should take care not to stay silent. If he possesses an abundance of wealth, he should watch out that he does not become sluggish in his generous works of mercy. If he possesses the art of wielding power, he should strive earnestly to use it for his neighbor. If he is in the position to speak directly to a rich man, he should fear damna-

---

[4] Prov. 1:5.
[5] Luke 21:1–4.

tion for not putting his talent to use by failing to intercede on behalf of the poor when the opportunity arises.[6]

In other words, through words and speech one can render a great service to beggars in need. Following Ecclesiasticus, "The rich man was the wrongdoer, yet continues to rage, but the poor man was wronged and will remain silent."[7] And Isidore is quoted in the *Decretum Gratiani* as saying, "Since a poor man has no bribes to offer in court, he will not only be despised and remain unheard. He will also be oppressed, against the truth."[8] In protecting the poor, you imitate God, for according to Job, patron of the poor, "God rescues the poor from the grip of the violent."[9] David also confirms that "God stands at the right hand of the poor, saving their souls from their persecutors."[10] On that account, in a matter of such importance to the Christian religion—where the lives of the poor and the souls of the rich are at stake—you cannot neglect your duty without incurring immediate punishment. This is what happened in the Gospel parable: a master severely rebuked his wicked and disloyal servant because he buried his talent underground.[11] Instead, he should have lent it, increased its value through interest, and then returned more than what he received.

I do not intend to condemn anyone by saying this. All people assuming the responsibility of defending the interests of the poor are guided by pious and religious zeal, whatever side they are on. In fact, a rich reward from God awaits both sides. The very thrust of my words is that everyone should publicly bring forward arguments related to this topic in accordance with their own ability and judgment. These arguments will allow both sides to discuss the topic and delineate

---

[6] Gregory the Great, *XL Homiliarum in Evangelia* I, hom. 9.7 (PL 76:1109).

[7] Ecclesiasticus 13:4.

[8] Isidore, Dec. Grat. C.11 q.3 c.72.

[9] Job 5:15.

[10] Ps. 108:31.

[11] Ed. note: The parable of the talents is in Matt. 25:14–30 and Luke 19:11–27.

the issue more precisely. Regarding my decision to address this plea to Your Greatness, I could not, or at least should not, have chosen another legitimate judge with whom to plead the cause of the poor apart from the emperor himself. First of all, God, "by whom kings reign and lawgivers decree just things,"[12] often and repeatedly calls himself Judge, Patron, Protector, and Father of the Poor, and regards those titles as seals of honor. As a result, the Fifth Council of Carthage admonished prelates to demand from the imperial power that it would assume patronship over the poor.[13] Second, this affair has already been brought before the imperial council a long time ago.

I have put my ideas to writing in both Latin and Spanish. The Latin version is more extended and concise at the same time. But I also drafted a Spanish version[14] for the following reasons. First, in speaking to princes we ought to use their mother tongue, even though Your Highness is proficient in both languages. As I remember, I have explained this to Your Highness when you deemed it worthy to honor our University of Salamanca by attending some of our lectures. Second, this affair about which I am going to speak concerns the people at large.[15] Since it is also in their interest to take notice of the affair, it has been worthwhile to talk about it in a language which they understand as well.

---

[12] Prov. 8:15.

[13] Ed. note: Dec. Grat. C.23 q.3 c.10. Cf. *Capitula concilii quinti Carthaginensis*, ch. 9 (PL 130:351).

[14] Ed. note: See Translators' Note, p. xlv n1.

[15] *causa popularis*.

2

Outline of the Events

The foundation stone, so to speak, on which the entire building of this affair rests is the illustrious petition number 46 addressed to the Royal Cortes of Valladolid in 1523.[1] It files a complaint with the emperor about the poor, accusing them of transgressing the borders of their homeland in order to go and beg all across the kingdom. Allegedly, the republic suffered many damages from the wandering about of those vagrant people. Therefore, justice was requested from the emperor in order to keep the beggars within their land of origin and prohibit them from wandering about. Although the response from the king was that he would see to it, his decision at that time was not published in any public edict.

---

[1] *Petitio illa fuit 46* [sic]… *in conventu regni valeolaetano anno* [1]523. Ed. note: Cortes of Valladolid, Petition 66 (Nueva Recopilación 1.12.6–9; Novísima Recopilación 7.39.1–13).

Therefore, a new complaint concerning vagrant beggars was filed through petition number 45 in the Cortes of Madrid in 1528.[2] However, the procurators[3] did not report a different response.

Then through petition number 117 in the Cortes of Madrid in 1534,[4] a supplication of a different nature was made, namely, that in each city of the kingdom the care of the poor should be entrusted to a prudent and cautious man. Without a positive testimonial and written permission from that man, no one must be allowed to beg from door to door. In this manner, the legitimate poor can be identified. The emperor accepted this supplication, meaning that vagabonds considered in good health by the law must be expelled from the towns, and foreigners begging under the false pretense of poverty[5] and hence without any right cannot stay at the court. He added that the truly poor should be taken care of and fed in their own dioceses. Nevertheless on this occasion, no penalty for the legitimate poor was decreed, no matter what region in the kingdom they had migrated to for the sake of begging.

Finally in 1540, the previously mentioned petitions were passed into law by the Royal Council.[6] This law, which is actually a decree by the

---

[2] *in conventu itidem celebrato Matriti anno* [1]*528 petitione 45*. Ed. note: Cortes of Valladolid, 1528, Petition 45 (Nueva Recopilación 1.12.6–9; Novísima Recopilación 7.39.1–13).

[3] Ed. note: The Spanish text of 1545 (Soto, *Relecciones y opúsculos*, II-2, 213) states that the original complaint of 1523 had also been filed by *procuratores* or *Procuradores*. According to Eduoard Fernandez-Bollo, the *procuradores* were representatives of eighteen cities in Castille and Léon that had the right to petition the king. Domingo de Soto, *La cause des pauvres*, trans. E. Fernandez-Bollo (Paris: Dalloz, 2013), 27n2.

[4] *in conventu, qui anno* [1]*534 eodem coactus est, petitione 117*. Ed. note: Cortes of Madrid, 1534, Petition 117 (Nueva Recopilación 1.12.6–9; Novísima Recopilación 7.39.1–13).

[5] Ed. note: The Spanish text reads "under pretext of pilgrimage." Soto, *Relecciones y opúsculos*, II-2, 213: "*so color de romero.*"

[6] *anno* [15]*40 curia, quae est Caesari a consilio ea ... senatus consulto edixit*. Ed. note: Decree by Emperor Charles V, 24 August 1540 (Nueva

Royal Council,[7] is extremely pertinent to our discussion, especially considering that a certain kind of instruction,[8] signed solely by the clerk,[9] was added right after the signatures of the members of the Royal Council. This instruction details the modalities of execution of the decree. Essentially, it consists of six articles:

First of all, we have to make sure that nobody is allowed to beg before his poverty is established by lawful examination. Second, no beggar, even if he is legitimate, is ever free to beg outside of his native land, and even there only within certain limits, except at times of extreme famine or other great calamity. Third, no one can beg without written permission either from the parish priest or from the person to whom that responsibility has been entrusted. Fourth, such written permission can only be granted to persons who have first confessed their sins through the sacrament of penance. Fifth, those who make a pilgrimage to the house of Saint James[10] are prohibited from making a long stop on their way and from deviating from the correct path for more than twelve miles (which we Spaniards call four leagues). The other provisions are very just and legitimate.[11] A sixth and final article orders diocesan and urban officials[12] to provide, to the best of

---

Recopilación 1.12.6–9; Novísima Recopilación 7.39.1–13). More references in Soto, *Relecciones y opúsculos*, II-2, 214n27.

[7] *senatusconsultum.*

[8] *instructio.*

[9] Ed. note: i.e., the *tabelio* (sic) in the Latin text, or the *escrivano de Cámara* in the Spanish text (Soto, *Relecciones y opúsculos*, II-2, 215), an important royal secretary. Fernandez-Bollo notes that this secretary, as an executor, possessed no authority of his own, enabling Soto to attack all articles only signed by him. Soto, *La cause des pauvres*, 28n1.

[10] Ed. note: The pilgrimage to Santiago de Compostela.

[11] *Reliqua iustissime sancita sunt.* Ed. note: The Spanish text reads: "*Todas las otras cosas que allí se añadieron fueron sanctas y buenas. E no tienen necessidad de más examinación*" (Soto, *Relecciones y opúsculos*, II-2, 215).

[12] The Latin text uses the rather general terminology "*dioecesani praetoresque urbium.*" These are, as we learn from the original Spanish text, "*los provisores y los corregidores*" (Soto, *Relecciones y opúsculos*, II-2, 215).

their ability, for the reform of the hospices, especially by reclaiming endowments from those owing and withholding them. Those officials should also make sure, to the extent possible, that the poor receive sufficient support in their own region, lest deprivation compel them to wander through strange lands. Last year, in 1544, this decree was published in Medina.

Building on this foundation, cities have begun to draft their own regulations. They state the following: First, vagabonds should be expelled from the city. Second, foreign beggars, upon their recovery and after receiving a modest amount of support, should be forced to leave immediately. Finally, native beggars should not be allowed to wander from door to door but should stay at home, while citizens charged with this public task should collect alms on their behalf and distribute them.

In order to execute these public tasks, several administrators, including praetors,[13] were appointed. All of this was surrounded with holy and pious zeal and with the intent to ensure that the legitimate poor might receive greater support. After all, out of shame they preferred to suffer severely in isolation inside their homes rather than going out to beg in public.[14]

When a little later people at our University of Salamanca started to grumble about such regulations, many of us were consulted by the city of Zamora. We did not applaud the articles without distinction, but we were able to promise that if several of them would be omitted in accordance with our judgment, we would sign the remaining articles. After a couple of days, the city of Zamora sent me a selection of articles that I was to sign. I have to be honest and admit my naivete and ignorance. I believed the writings only contained the articles for which I had given

---

[13] *praetores*. Ed. note: In the Spanish text we read, "*mayordomos y diputados y alguaziles*" (Soto, *Relecciones y opúsculos*, II-2, 217).

[14] Ed. note: Here a short passage from the original edition of 1545 (Soto, *Relecciones y opúsculos*, II-2, 216–17) was omitted in the new edition of 1547. In it, Soto praised the moral character of Diego de Toledo, the Prior of the Order of Saint John in Castile, who resided in Zamora and played an important role in reforming Zamora's poor relief policy. Soto repeatedly states that he does not want to doubt the intentions and "pious zeal" of those who had been active in reforming the poor relief policy.

approval by word of mouth, and so it occurred that I signed the text without reading it. It is not as if my signature, put alongside that of so many famous experts, made any difference in terms of authority, but still, I understand now that the text contained a number of articles which I would not have approved of so naively had I read them first. I am saying this because in those days the Most Reverend Cardinal of Toledo asked me in Valladolid to deliver my opinion on the issue of almsgiving. Since I said that I did not agree with everything that was happening, people objected by showing the articles of the city of Zamora, duly signed by me. I understand that supporters of these articles later also produced them before Your Highness.

But as far as I am concerned, I do not consider myself as possessing the authority that the Pythagoreans attributed to Pythagoras, who demanded no proof beyond the words of their master. Rather, I wish that the rule laid down by Augustine in one of his letters to Jerome and included in the *Decretum* was applied to everyone who speaks on this subject and especially to myself, namely, that with the exception of the canonical books, we should trust no author more than his power of reasoning and persuasion allow, however great his holiness and erudition.[15] Therefore, whatever I might have signed at one time or another bears almost no relevance. If asked about the truth of the matter, I would rather call to witness all the reasons and arguments written down in this little treatise.

To return to the core of the matter,[16] the city of Salamanca has now adopted the same regulations as Zamora, although they met with opposition. The regulations have now also reached Valladolid, allegedly leaving you perplexed, Most Serene Lord, and not without reason. It therefore came to my mind to write this deliberation to Your Greatness, whatever its merits. This outline of events might have been too long, but it seemed necessary to me to provide a complete summary of the affair before entering into the details.

---

[15] Dec. Grat. Dist.9. c.5.

[16] *Indiverticulum itaque ut revertar.* Ed. note: Literally, "To return to our digression," but we have made use of the text of 1545. Soto, *Relecciones y opúsculos*, II-2, 218: "*Ad rem itaque ut revertar.*"

3

ON VAGABONDS

It is worthwhile to divide this deliberation, as any other subject of consultation, into two parts. First, we should establish what is lawful and what is unlawful. Next, among what it is lawful, we have to examine what can be considered expedient. Thus the basic division that is implicit in the apostle Paul's words in the first epistle to the Corinthians: "All things are lawful to me, but not all things are expedient. All things are lawful to me, but not all things are edifying."[1] A single method to scrutinize both parts does not exist. Whether something is lawful has to be examined and weighed differently from whether something is expedient. For what is lawful must be done as a matter of law. There is no room for debate about something laid down in a written law, as can be derived from the law *Prospeximus* in the Digest.[2] But whenever two things are licit according to law, and we are deliberating which of them is the more expedient, a conclusion must be reached from the principle of what is equitable and good[3] and from arguments based on prudence.

---

[1] 1 Cor. 6:12; 10:23.

[2] Dig. 40.9.12.

[3] *ex aequo et bono.*

Since the matter can be clarified by making a distinction, it is important to distinguish between vagabonds and people who wander and beg throughout the world because they are truly in need. With regard to the first class of men, it has been determined not only by a particular law of the kingdom, but also by the much older common law[4] as well as by divine and natural law that they should not be allowed to dwell with impunity in the territory of our state. The second class of men, however, that is, the foreigners and the pilgrims, have not been condemned by any law for wandering around anywhere—at least as far as I can see and unless greater experts in jurisprudence say otherwise. Moreover, if we heed the suggestions of natural reason, condemning the second class of people is apparently at variance with the principle of the equitable and good, and if we consult the gospel, it is irreconcilable with Christian charity.

The Term "Vagabond"

Regarding the first group of people, the "vagabonds," their name seems at first glance to refer to nothing but men who roam the world without having a fixed home or domicile.[5] Nevertheless, to understand the correct meaning of the word, we should add that these men wander about uselessly and pointlessly without being driven by necessity. Otherwise the name "vagabond" would not be as infamous as it obviously is, denoting idle men. Therefore, those who leave their native land in order to practice a profession or to conduct business or for any other useful or necessary reason are not the subject of reproach, nor are they being denoted by the infamous name of "vagrancy."

---

[4] *lex communis*. Ed. note: This term refers to the *ius commune*, the Roman legal tradition that constituted the shared legal heritage of civil and canon law in late medieval and early modern Europe. See M. Bellomo, *The Common Legal Past of Europe, 1000–1800* (Washington, DC: Catholic University of America Press, 1995).

[5] See the jurists' interpretation of the final chapter of *De foro competenti* and the law *Haeres absens*. Ed. note: Dec. Greg. 2.2.20 and Dig. 5.1.19.1–2. For the terms "vagabond" (*vagabundus*), "beggar" (*mendicus*), and "poor" (*pauper*), see also the definitions given in ch. 12.

Vagrancy Is Forbidden by Divine Law

Such men should not be allowed to wander around with impunity. For it is not as though they had enough financial means to allow themselves to stay away from servile work.[6] Nor are they weak or suffering from any other kind of impairment that would prevent them from undertaking hard labor.

The first argument for this proposition is based on divine law. God warned us against this at the beginning of the newly created world, when he cast man out of very pleasant Paradise, giving him his due punishment. If only man had persevered in faith and equity, he would have continued to enjoy the sweetest leisure of contemplation!

But God said to us, "By the sweat of your brow will you eat bread."[7] And afterwards he confirmed this in the form of a figure of speech when he said in Deuteronomy: "You shall not muzzle the ox while he is treading."[8] According to Paul's interpretation of this passage in his first epistle to the Corinthians, this does not express so much the care that God has for cattle as that men who labor and work are deserving of the bread they eat.[9] Those who are idle, however, are not in the least worthy of it. And Christ himself, our Savior, considered the laborer worthy of his pay[10] when he reprimanded—through the mouth of the head of the family[11]—men standing idle in the marketplace, even though they were able to excuse their idleness by saying that no one had been willing to hire them.[12] And in the second epistle to the Thessalonians, Paul bitterly reproved some brothers in Christ who, while evading all work and labor, nevertheless continued to receive alms from the people. He concluded that "he who does not work, will

---

[6] *opera servilia*.

[7] Gen. 3:19.

[8] Deut. 25:4.

[9] 1 Cor. 9:9.

[10] Matt. 10:10.

[11] *paterfamilias*.

[12] Matt. 20:6–7.

not eat."[13] There are some men who are—to avoid using worse terms to describe them—reckless and imprudent in their speech and have tried to read that passage as an attack on mendicant monks. But in this passage and elsewhere, Paul publicly taught that those who sow spiritual seeds are legally entitled to reap the fruits in terms of temporal goods.[14] However, this is not the place for a digression on the exegesis of that passage.[15] We should rather return to the discussion of our proposition.

Vagrancy Is Forbidden by Natural Law

The conclusion that vagrancy is forbidden is also proven by natural reason. A person without enough means to survive has no right to claim other people's goods unless he is willing to serve those people with his talents, efforts, or enterprise. In this state of fallen nature, God wisely provided for us humans in both ways, namely, by having both rich and poor people. The rich should be like the soul which governs the body; the poor like the body which serves the soul. The poor are supposed to cultivate the earth and exercise mechanical arts,[16] providing labor without which human life cannot be sustained. As Aristotle confirms, God and nature have never created anything in vain.[17] Therefore, those who spend their life in idleness live without respect for the law of nature. It is almost as if idle people do not exist, as Seneca and Cicero write.[18] Demetrius the Philosopher even called

---

[13] 2 Thess. 3:10.

[14] Ed. note: e.g., 1 Cor. 9:11.

[15] Ed. note: For an analysis of the seminal impact of Paul's adage "he who does not work, will not eat" (2 Thess. 3:10) on Western economic thought, see S. Piron, *Généalogie de la morale économique* (Brussels: Zones Sensibles, 2020), 43, 181–86.

[16] *artes mechanicae*.

[17] Aristotle, *De natura animalium* X. Ed. note: Aristotle, *De incessu animalium* 2 (704b) and 8 (708a).

[18] Seneca, *Epistulae ad Lucilium* XIX; Cicero, *De natura deorum* II.

idle men "a sea of dead people."[19] As a consequence, even high-ranking and powerful people who claim taxes from their subjects cannot do so with any right unless they show care and skill in governing their subjects, even if that requires hard labor and sweat. As our emperor knows very well, thanks to his long experience in most illustriously managing the affairs of state, and as you, Famous Prince, have already begun to experience, princes also have the full and entire right to be paid taxes by the republic, but only insofar as they support the numerous and huge burdens of government: "to protect the republic by leading the armed forces, to adorn it by imposing high moral standards and to punish and correct its members through law and justice," as the famous poet Horace says.[20]

Idleness Is Evil

The third reason for the aforementioned conclusion is the following: "Idleness[21] has taught much evil,"[22] as Solomon says.[23] Through another proverb he explains why this is the case: Since an idle person is always pregnant with desires, to what else can he give birth besides malice and iniquity?[24] First of all, the habit of claiming goods from

---

[19] Ed. note: Demetrius as cited by Seneca, *Epistulae ad Lucilium* VII, ep. 67.14.

[20] *ut ait ille*. Ed. note: Horace, *Epistulae* II, ep. 1, v. 1–4. The notion, famously expressed by Horace in his address to Augustus, that leadership consists of wielding arms, improving morals, and maintaining order through laws became a commonplace in ancient, medieval, and early modern political philosophy. See P. Mastandrea, "*Armis et legibus*. Un motto attribuito a Iamblichus nei *Romana* di Iordanes," *Incontri triestini di filologia classica* 5 (2005–2006): 315–28 (here 317–18).

[21] *ociositas*.

[22] Ed. note: Ecclesiasticus 33:29.

[23] Ed. note: Traditionally Ecclesiasticus has been attributed to Sirach, not Solomon. The attribution to Solomon might have originated from a mix-up between Ecclesiasticus and Ecclesiastes.

[24] Ed. note: Prov. 21:25–26. The Proverbs (*Parabolae Salamonis*) have traditionally been attributed to Solomon.

others is directly tied to the vice of flattery. Second, the idle person loses his feelings of shame, that bridle by which men are restrained from plunging into the abyss of their vices. Third, his flesh and body become too weak to resist lust. As a famous poet wrote, "by taking away idleness, you break the bow of Cupid."[25] Fourth, begging teaches the false poor how to steal. In sum, since men of better repute who would have inspired them with their good morals do not keep their company or have any dealings with those wicked men, they easily forget all tenets of the Christian faith. Moreover, once they have been infected with this evil complexion, they contaminate and corrupt others. That is why Plato considers idleness in his *Republic* akin to a plague.[26] Hence, he took the greatest care that no one in his republic would live a life of idleness. Among our holy theologians, Jerome strongly reminded us that we are protected by a shield against the weapons of the devil as long as he does not find us in a state of idleness.[27] Augustine says in a certain letter to the people of Vercelli, "Idleness brings forth no fruit, but losses. The idle Esau lost the blessing of his primogeniture, because he preferred to receive food rather than work to earn it."[28] In his commentary on the Gospel of John, Chrysostom says that "we have been perverted by idleness; by refraining to work we have been corrupted."[29] Seneca affirms that "idleness weakens one's bodily strength, just like rust weakens iron. The fire of a torch loses its intensity if the torch is not moved, but once stirred, the fire regains its strength."[30] And this is what the prophet Ezekiel said upon rebuking the inhabitants of Jerusalem, revealing the origins of every evil: "This was the iniquity of

---

[25] Ed. note: Ovidius, *Remedia amoris* 139.

[26] Ed. note: It is not clear which passage in Plato's *Republic* Soto is referencing.

[27] Dec. Grat. *De consecr.* Dist.5 c.33 [Jerome, ep. 125.11 (PL 22:1078)].

[28] Ed. note: This quote stems not from Augustine but from Ambrose. See Ambrose, ep. 63 (PL 16:1216). The story of Esau's loss of his birthright can be found in Gen. 25.

[29] Ed. note: Chrysostom, *Homilia in Joannem* 38.2 (PG 59:205).

[30] Seneca, *De Clementia*.

your sister Sodom: pride, satiation with bread, abundance and idleness were in her and her daughters, and they did not give a helping hand to the needy and the poor."[31]

Instructed by these testimonies and arguments, many have contributed to the construction of the republic, either through writing or direct involvement in its administration. But they were always committed to the same idea, namely, that idle men must be removed from the republic since such men are "vinegar to the teeth, and smoke to the eyes."[32]

In his *Politics*, Aristotle divided the people of the republic into men of leisure and men of work.[33] He ordered men with superior intellectual qualities to belong to the class of men of leisure, also calling them "free men." They should be exempt from mechanical arts[34] and any other kind of physical labor. Some of them should sit at the helm of the state or be put in charge of military affairs. Others should concentrate on the study of literature, and a final group should devote themselves to divine worship. By contrast, no leisure should be given to the common folk who are servile and whose capability lies more in their bodily strength than in their mental prowess. Rather, they ought to be always kept busy and at work. For this reason, the Lacedaemonians, men fierce in war, trained their youth in arms and military affairs, perhaps even too much so.[35] Numa Pompilius, the second king of the Romans and a man inclined toward religion and peace, established a multitude of religious ceremonies and sacrifices. As Livy recounts,[36] he did so not only to worship the gods, but also to avoid idleness among his soldiers.

---

[31] Ezek. 16:49.

[32] According to a saying by King Solomon. Ed. note: Prov. 10:26.

[33] Aristotle, *Politica* VII. Ed. note: especially VII, 7–9 (1328a–30a).

[34] Ed. note: *mechanicae artes*, as opposed to the *artes liberales*.

[35] As the Philosopher explains in the same book. Ed. note: Aristotle, *Politica* VII, 13 (1333b–34a).

[36] Ed. note: Livy, *Ab Urbe Condita* I, 19–21.

Vagrancy Is Also Forbidden by Common Law

Let us go on and examine the question from the point of view of the common law.[37] Emperor Justinian laid down a law on vagrancy in the eleventh book of the Code, which he gave the title "On able-bodied beggars."[38] This title treats of those who are not only in good health but also strong enough to work and yet feign and simulate infirmity to beg and wander around the world. They harm the legitimate poor by usurping alms destined to them. By virtue of Justinian's law, anyone has the power and authority to take ownership[39] of vagabonds, provided that they have the status of slaves. If the vagabonds are in fact free citizens, they can be claimed as peasants working the land for the rest of their lives.[40] Almost exactly the same rule can be retrieved in the *Authenticum* "On the quaestor."[41] It provides that the quaestor is responsible for investigating the foreigners in the city, verifying what kind of people they are and what business or fortune brought them into the city. He should attend to their affairs that they might be easily dealt with. If they want to stay and they are in good health, they should be compelled to work. If they are of servile status, they should be handed over to their owners.

Vagrancy Is Forbidden by Castilian Law

More specific laws for this kingdom have been derived from the common law.[42] After all, never did the ancestors of Your Highness decree anything on this topic which was not intended to be in accordance with the common law. The first legal provision is included in the *Siete*

---

[37] *ius commune*. Ed. note: see p. 18n4.

[38] Cod. 11.26.

[39] *manu capere*.

[40] *perpetuus colonatus*. Ed. note: On the difference between "free" peasants (*coloni*) and slaves in late imperial Roman law, see B. Sirks, "The Colonate in the Later Roman Empire," *Legal History Review* 90 (2022): forthcoming.

[41] *Authenticum De quaestore colla.* 6. Ed. note: Nov. 80.3–4.

[42] *ius commune*.

Partidas.[43] It corresponds to Justinian's "On able-bodied beggars." It provides that vagabonds and "sobeiani"—the legal term used in the *Siete Partidas*—have to be repelled from the republic like enemies. This has also been enacted in a different law of greater length, a law of the so-called *Ordenamiento* which was promulgated in Briviesca in 1387.[44] It makes reference to another kind of damage incurred by the republic due to the vagabonds, new in comparison to what we have already mentioned above. As long as that mob of idle men is allowed, the fields are not being cultivated by workers, and the republic suffers from a lack of craftsmen. Although the severity of the punishment imposed on vagrants by the law "On able-bodied beggars" has been moderated, this law still gives anyone the power to force a vagabond into personal servitude[45] for a whole month, without the need to pay him a salary, as long as basic sustenance is provided. Either that or he shall be beaten with whips and expelled from the city.

All of this, Most Perfect Prince, has been laid down inviolably with regard to the expulsion of the vagabonds, both by divine and natural law, and thereupon by positive law as well, both in the common law and the kingdom's particular law. As I see it, our first conclusion has now been sufficiently established and confirmed. Indeed, beggars who are able-bodied should not be tolerated, just as the emperor has frequently and prudently commanded by public edict, both at the Cortes of Madrid in 1534[46] and elsewhere.

---

[43] *Extat primum inter eas, quas partitarum vocant: parte ii titulo xx edictum.* Ed. note: *Siete Partidas* 2.20.4. The *Siete Partidas* is the famous Castilian law code compiled during the reign of King Alfonso in the thirteenth century.

[44] *Lex prima est tituli. 14 lib. 8 Birviescae anno [1]387 promulgata.* Ed. note: Nueva Recopilación 8.11.1.

[45] *servitium*.

[46] *Caesar in conventu apud Matritum anno [15]34.* Ed. note: Cortes of Madrid, 1534, Petition 117 (Nueva Recopilación 1.12.6–9; Novísima Recopilación 7.39.1–13).

4

ON FOREIGN BEGGARS

We can now go on and consider the second part of the division which we previously made. We now have to ask the question whether it is licit for a man who is not falsely but truly poor to leave the borders of his homeland without means and wander throughout the kingdom for the purpose of begging. Or on the contrary, if such people can be confined by law within the borders of their homeland, as is stipulated by the above-mentioned petitions. Had a law concerning the topic already been promulgated by the emperor, and had it been received through long use, I would have been afraid to speak out—even though, if it had been expedient, the Most Equitable Emperor and Wisest Court would still have been willing to change the law. For we do not do injustice to the laws by adapting them to the changing times. Moreover, the law that we are talking about was never enforced. In fact, if you carefully look at the decree[1] of 1540, it was not even meant to be a law. As a result, I take it that I am just rendering a service by giving Your Highness an overview of the following arguments against the validity of the decree.

---

[1] *senatusconsultum.*

The Petitions Are a Novelty

First of all, those petitions are so new[2] that no such law has ever been proposed or enacted in any nation. I certainly do not assert this rashly, but I call all divine and human laws to witness. This is, of course, a very strong and valid argument against this new invention. For believe me, Most Renowned Prince, that if the invention had followed so clearly as they claim from what is equitable and good, ancient laws would already exist prescribing those measures. Yet both the common law and the particular law of the kingdom admonish the opposite, as do natural reason and Sacred Scripture.

The *Authenticum* "On the quaestor"

The *Authenticum* "On the quaestor"[3] stipulates that the business of foreigners should be thoroughly controlled, specifying that once it has been dealt with, all healthy and strong foreigners are to be sent back to their respective native land or compelled to work. But then the law goes on and makes the following exception: "We order that sick or old persons, regardless of their sex, should be allowed to remain in our city without being disturbed." Here, absolutely no distinction was made between natives and foreigners.

The *Ordenamiento*

The law which we Spanish call the *Ordenamiento*[4] (to which I referred earlier) concurs with the provisions in the *Authenticum*. It first ordered to send vagabonds into exile, but then makes an exception for the old, the sick, and the disabled. On the basis of their appearance alone it is licit to assume that they cannot sustain themselves through physical work or labor. Without making any distinction between citizens and foreigners, this law allows them to beg with impunity. King Henry II

---

[2] *res nova*.

[3] Ed. note: Nov. 80, 5.

[4] *Lex quam hispani dicimus ordinamenti*. Ed. note: Nueva Recopilación 8.11.1. More references in Soto, *Relecciones y opúsculos*, II-2, 234n31.

has confirmed the validity of this law by virtue of a *ley de Toro*.[5] Consequently, I cannot understand how one could infer from such common and particular laws that borders and limits should be imposed on the beggars, outside of which they are not free to beg for alms. After all until now, no single law had discriminated between locals and foreigners, as long as they were poor. Rather, the laws made a distinction between the false, feigned beggars and the legitimate ones. If I am allowed to conjecture about this, His Imperial Majesty and His Royal Council delayed their definitive response to supplications of this kind for seventeen years because they questioned whether the supplications were really inspired by a Christian attitude toward the truly poor rather than by annoyance at the beggars' presence. The response to petition 117 at the Cortes of Madrid[6] in 1534 cannot be cited to the contrary, for it only speaks about vagabonds in stating that they should suffer the punishment of the law. With respect to the legitimate needy, the emperor added that they should be taken care of in their respective dioceses. That is more demonstrative of the king's clemency than of the severity of the law. By making his response conditional, stating that they are not allowed to beg if their needs are sufficiently provided for, he made a just decree because he did not distinguish between foreigners and natives. In truth, the only thing the council of the year 1540 wanted to ordain was that the poor should not be allowed to beg if and only if it is established with certitude that all they need was amply available to them at home.[7] Yet never has it been decreed that beggars of proven legitimacy[8] should be punished for going wherever they wanted to beg for alms.

---

[5] *Hentricus rex apud Taurum edicto novo*. Ed. note: Nueva Recopilación 8.11.1–2. More references in Soto, *Relecciones y opúsculos*, II-2, 234n36.

[6] *responsum ad petitionem 117 in conventu apud Mattitum* [sic] *anno* [15]34. Ed. note: Novísima Recopilación 7.39.1–13; Nueva Recopilación 1.12.6–9.

[7] *curia anno* [15]40. Ed. note: Nueva Recopilación 1.12.6–19; Novísima Recopilación 7.39.1–13. More references in Soto, *Relecciones y opúsculos*, II-2, 236n57.

[8] *probati mendici*.

Conclusion: The Truly Poor Can Rightfully Beg Anywhere

On condition that more knowledgeable experts approve it, here is our conclusion. Poor people who are truly in need cannot be expelled from any place. Just as natives and residents, foreign beggars should either be allowed to beg, or they should be sustained in another way. Inasmuch as my abilities allow, however limited they are, I can corroborate this conclusion by adducing five or six arguments.

Argument 1

If we leave the testimonies which I would take from Holy Scripture out of consideration, the first argument is the following: except for public enemies, conspirators against the republic, and criminals, nobody can be excluded from any city. The reason is self-evident. According to natural law and the law of nations, roads and cities ought to be open to everyone without distinction. Nobody can be deprived of the right to stay where he wants unless he is committing a sin.[9] That is why exile is counted among the harsh punishments of the law. The Law *Capitalium* from Justinian's Digest[10] states that even though exile is not a capital punishment altogether, it is at least thought of as coming close to one. And although sending back a foreigner to his own land does not constitute the most severe form of exile, it nevertheless remains a violation of the right which gives everyone the power[11] to spend his life where he wishes. Since those who are considered poor beyond any doubt commit absolutely no crime or offense by begging, they can never be lawfully expelled from a city or town as long as they want to stay there.

Argument 2

The second reason is perhaps more obvious. Princely authorities and the republic cannot make positive laws with regard to alms that

---

[9] *culpa.*
[10] Dig. 48.19.28.
[11] *facultas.*

are more burdensome for the citizens than the laws of nature and the gospel. Let me explain myself. There is a dispute among theologians because some teach that the precept to give alms by virtue of divine and natural law is not binding under pain of mortal sin unless the beggar is suffering extreme necessity. Others, however, have concluded with more certitude that someone is not only bound to give alms under pain of mortal sin when confronted with a person in extreme necessity, but also whenever he has, according to his rank and condition, an abundance of goods, and the beggar is suffering at least from serious[12] necessity. The latter opinion is in accordance with Saint Thomas and others.[13] But perhaps even in that case, nobody is under an absolute obligation to give alms to this or that particular person at any given moment. It may be enough to give, every now and then, from one's own surpluses to any needy person. The prince cannot add any further obligation to those laws except for the fact that in cases of extreme necessity, he can compel his citizens to observe the laws by threatening them with sanctions. Beyond that case, however, he cannot force his citizens to give alms by punishing them. The reason is that this would go beyond the scope of the evangelical precept which is only binding under mortal sin in the above-mentioned cases. Paul says that "everyone should give what he has determined in his heart to give, not out of sadness or of necessity: for God loves a cheerful giver."[14]

Even those who are not in extreme or serious necessity nevertheless have the right to beg for alms in order to alleviate their plight. Assisting those people is a matter of practicing the virtuous office of mercy. When the emperor and his council proclaimed that the poor should be supported in their own territory, they did not intend to compel citizens by force to provide the poor with such ample support that they would no longer want to beg. Rather, they wanted the endowments of hospices to be reclaimed from those who owe them. Without laying down an enforceable precept, they added that diocesan

---

[12] *in gravi saltem necessitate.*

[13] Ed. note: Thomas Aquinas, *Summa theologiae* II-2, q. 32, a. 5.

[14] Ed. note: 2 Cor. 9:7.

and urban officials should do their best to make sure that the poor are relieved in their own homes if a way exists to make this possible.

From this I derive yet another argument.[15] No one, however great his authority or power may be, can prevent the poor from leaving their settlements in order to beg unless he puts his citizens under a legal obligation, beyond the virtue of mercy, to feed and clothe the poor and administer the things which they need. For if he confined the poor in a more severe way than he urged the rich to open their purses, he would compel the miserable to expose themselves to extreme suffering. No prince can compel citizens so forcefully to feed beggars—and, in fact, it has not happened before. Consequently, neither can he force beggars to stay in their own land. Even if a harsh law were enacted compelling the bishops to feed the poor on pain of severe sanctions, the citizens would nevertheless not be able to provide for everyone, leaving the needy free to ignore the law and go wherever they want in order to beg. For I ask, How can the law prohibit the miserable from leaving their native land? That is not a crime or a sin. How could that be sinful if there is no other way to provide for their basic needs and those of their families?

Argument 3

The third argument can help explain the previous one with more clarity. Just like some are rich and others are poor within the walls of a single city, within the boundaries of a single diocese there are some towns abounding in riches and good fortune and others that are plagued by poverty and need. In the same way, in the entire kingdom there are some very rich dioceses either because the soil is more fertile there and the earth more favorable to fruit-bearing or because the people became more affluent through trade. Some dioceses, however, are barren and poor. For this reason, just as the rich citizens should support the poor of the same city with alms, so the more prosperous

---

[15] Ed. note: The Latin text expressly mentions that this is the second argument (*secunda ratio*), both in the main text and in the margin. However, this must be an editorial mistake, considering that the previous argument, too, is cited as the second one (*secunda ratio*).

towns should support the poorer towns in the same diocese (as is conceded by the authors of these petitions). In the same way, affluent dioceses cannot expel poor foreigners coming from barren regions. The reason behind the analogy is obvious. The entire kingdom constitutes a single body and a single republic just like any city or province. The cities are like the members of that republic. Just think, Wisest Prince, about why God placed the rich and fertile region of Tierra de Campos next to the borders of Asturia and its mountainous regions—a rocky, barren, and infertile piece of land—and then added the Kingdom of Toledo to it? Did he not do that to compensate the poverty of some areas with the fertility of the others? This mechanism does not only apply when there is a famine or a great calamity, for not only the extremely poor suffer but also those who are poor though not in a situation of extreme necessity. To deal with their plight, they have the right to beg. Your Highness, why would the Royal Council of your kingdom which spends thousands of ducats not be ready to accept many more beggars than a small province? A single household of any prelate or magnate in your kingdom has enough means to feed more beggars than a hundred citizens would be capable of. Considering that miserable men of this sort are treated like worms in our state and trampled upon, let them at least be allowed to ascend the treetops with the ants in order to find their sustenance.

When shortly before I seemed to suggest that only one kingdom constituted a single body, I did so out of indulgence—to use Paul's words.[16] I would actually like to add that according to the law of Christ, the poor of one kingdom should have free access also to a different kingdom. The apostle taught the Corinthians that we are all members of a single body, and he did not want to reduce the scope of the metaphor to the narrowness of one kingdom. Rather, he said that we are "all baptized by one Spirit into one body."[17] Therefore it is not only one kingdom which constitutes a single body, but rather all of us as Christians are regenerated through our single baptism into

---

[16] Ed. note: 1 Cor. 7:6.

[17] 1 Cor. 12:13.

one body so that each and every one of us is mutually a member of the other, receiving a varied set of advantages and responsibilities.

In a Greek fable, a blind man carried a lame man on his shoulders so that the lame man might direct the steps of the blind man. In a similar fashion, those among the Christians who excel in intellect should be the eyes of the ignorant, while those who have the upper hand in bodily strength and vigor ought to be the hands and feet of the weak. But the rich who possess wealth in this world[18] should in turn serve as the stomach of the poor, providing them with what they need to live. Finally, Christ has to be at the head of all. Paul says in accordance with the gospel that "there is no distinction between Jew and Greek in Christ: for the same is Lord of all."[19] If we look even deeper into the matter and evaluate it according to the standards of natural law, we can state that by their very nature all mortals are connected to one another by a very close bond. Consequently, we would not even be allowed to expel unbelieving beggars from our republic unless they were public enemies or if we feared some detriment to our faith from them.

Argument 4

The fourth argument is the following. Besides the fact that some provinces are more prosperous than others, some people are generous to the poor while others show no mercy. And since men cannot be forced to give alms for any reason other than the one we have talked about before,[20] the poor would be cruelly maltreated if they were not granted the permission to move freely from one province to another. Next, the weak and the sick are affected by harmful air and often need to move to a region where they can recover in a healthier environment. It may well be that inhabitants of a city get fed up with the persistent and frequent begging of a poor person. In that case, or perhaps for

---

[18] Ed. note: 1 John 3:17.

[19] Rom. 10:12.

[20] Ed. note: i.e., if they are suffering under extreme necessity; cf. above, arg. 2, p. 31.

some other reason, he will be forced to change country again. Moreover, a person might have made enemies in his homeland, or he may have sinned or committed an offense for which he fears punishment. For all these reasons, he may be forced to move elsewhere as a deserter or a person in exile. It is not lawful to force a poor person any more than a rich individual to render account for deserting his homeland.

Argument 5

The fifth argument is derived from the right to hospitality. In fact, there never was a nation or republic in antiquity in which hospitality was not held in great esteem, and it was practiced by every religion. Plato made hospitality the third part of friendship.[21] Theophrastus exalted it with the highest praises, as reported by Cicero.[22] To honor Jupiter, whom they worshiped as the strongest and greatest among the gods, the pagans gave him the title "Hospitable." Under that name they erected temples and altars for Jupiter because he was supposed to be a most severe judge and vindicator of the violated right of guests.

But let us not only look for testimonies among the gentiles. Paul said to the Hebrews, "Do not forget hospitality: for thereby some have received angels as guests without being aware of it."[23] He alluded to the hospitality with which Abraham and Lot received angels,[24] thanks to which Lot and his family escaped the destruction of Sodom. God considered hospitality worthy of such great honor that he sent angels to earth in order to receive the good deed of hospitality. And Rahab, a prostitute in Jericho, was saved from the massacre and the sack of the city on account of a service of hospitality.[25] There are also many provisions of canon law in which guests are entrusted to the care of Christians. In other words, if the duty of hospitality has always been

---

[21] Ed. note: According to Prats, this could be a reference to Plato, *Lysis* 212a. Cf. Soto, *Relecciones y opúsculos*, II-2, 242n189.

[22] Ed. note: Cicero, *De officiis* II.18, 64.

[23] Heb. 13:2.

[24] Ed. note: Gen. 18:1–8; 19:1–3.

[25] Ed. note: Josh. 2.

held in such high regard, whom should Christians show their hospitality to if they want to receive the greatest praises and merit if not to the needy and beggars? Moreover, hospitality is exercised not so much toward our own citizens and inhabitants as toward foreigners and strangers. Although it is also a duty to take any person in need under one's roof, strictly speaking the word "hospitality" refers to helping foreigners. Finally, let us corroborate our conclusion with the words of the saints. Nowhere in Sacred Scripture do we find a distinction between native citizens and foreigners insofar as they are poor. Rather, both the Old and New Testaments commend with equal force poor foreigners and locals to our care, establishing the same right for both. First in Exodus 23, God says, "You shall not oppress a stranger, for you know what moves the hearts of strangers: for you were also strangers in the land of Egypt."[26] Then in Leviticus 23 he says, "When you shall reap the corn of your land, you shall not cut it to the ground: neither shall you gather the ears that remain. But you shall leave them for the poor and for the strangers."[27] And according to Deuteronomy 10, God "loves the stranger, and gives him food and raiment: and therefore you should love strangers."[28] And a little later in chapter 14, God says, "To the stranger who is within your gates, you either give it that he may eat, or you sell it to him."[29] You do the first if he is needy, and you do the second if he has the means to buy it. This is the most important of all the things which Christ our Savior warned us that he will demand an account for, namely, that when he came as a stranger and had no place to stay, we should have received him with hospitality.[30]

---

[26] Exod. 23:9.

[27] Lev. 23:22.

[28] Deut. 10:18–19.

[29] Ed. note: Deut. 14:21. The verse is cited incompletely; the object which should be given or sold to the foreigner is actually the meat of an animal that is "dead of itself" (Douay-Rheims 1899, American ed.).

[30] Ed. note: Matt. 25:35.

Therefore, let those who expel poor foreigners answer the following questions. If we expel vagabonds and are not hospitable to poor strangers, who will be left toward whom we can practice mercy? Perhaps they might mention illustrious and affluent men who receive hospitality among their equals. However, even though that is also a duty, I do not think that these men are the ones designated by Christ when he counted hospitality among the alms that we have to give to the poor.

Conclusion

So unless I am mistaken, my judgment is that the poor have a right to go to any place in the kingdom to beg, and that it is not enough to support them for two or three days in a city if they prefer to stay longer.

5

Refutation of the Objections

Never have I seen a law opposed to the above-mentioned principles, unless we consider a decree laid down in Ypres in Flanders as a true law. Among other regulations instituted in Ypres in a forward-looking and Christian manner, they have laid down a decree declaring that the city should not be open to poor foreigners.[1] Yet not every single example of a regulation should be considered as a universal law. They claim that experts from the University of Paris have given their approval for the decree,[2] but I could never believe that. The only thing they could have approved of is that the citizens of Ypres are not under an obligation to provide for all poor foreigners. The experts from Paris, or any other expert in the law or Holy Scriptures, could not possibly have approved of the prohibition for foreigners to enter the city, on any ground.

---

[1] Ed. note: On the regulations regarding poor foreigners, see J. Nolf, *La réforme de la bienfaisance publique à Ypres au XVIe siècle* (Ghent: Vander Haeghen, 1915), 14–18 et passim.

[2] Ed. note: Nolf, *La réforme*, 110, 119–33.

DELIBERATION ON THE CAUSE OF THE POOR

The Council of Tours

However, the strongest of all arguments by those who assert that the poor can be contained by law inside their native lands stems from the Second Council of Tours celebrated under Pope Pelagius I almost a thousand years ago.[3] It contains the following words in its fifth chapter: "Each and every city should provide its poor and needy inhabitants with sufficient nourishment in accordance with its own ability. Both priests and citizens should take care of feeding the poor in their own region. In this manner, the poor will not have to engage in tiresome traveling and dwell in foreign cities."[4] In reality, this most equitable and sacred decree is clearly more supportive of our view than of the opposite opinion. The provision from this council does not contain any prohibition for the poor to go wherever they want to beg. Rather, in the interest of the poor, the council urges each city to support its own poor citizens. In this manner, as the text of the council explains, the poor will not have to engage in tiresome traveling and dwell in foreign places. Furthermore, the text cannot be accused of novelty in saying that each and every city should feed its own poor citizens properly. The cities are just being admonished, in conformity with the truth of the gospel, to behave toward the poor in such a manner that the miserable are not forced to seek nourishment elsewhere.

At the time of the council, the poor could still count on great care from the prelates, the charity of their subjects, and the kindness of all. The poor were not only not at all required to go abroad; they did not even have to beg in their native land—unless the city was so poor, perhaps, that it had insufficient means to support its own beggars. We can frequently read this, especially in the writings of Saint Cyprian. Talking about a poor city, he wrote in one of his letters, "If the church over there is unable to provide the afflicted with nourishment, they

---

[3] Ed. note: The Second Council of Tours was held in 567.

[4] Ed. note: J. D. Mansi, ed., *Sacrorum Conciliorum nova et amplissima collectio*, vol. 9 (Florence: Antonius Zatta, 1763), 793.

can move to us in order that they may receive food and clothing here."[5] And in another letter he wrote, "May you, in the meantime, take care of the poor to the best of your ability, in order that the means to remove their need might be furnished by your diligence."[6] And consider the following text: "Please, take diligent care of the infirm and all the poor. And if some of the pilgrims should be in need, you may obtain what you need from my personal funds. Out of fear that they might have been fully spent already, I have sent another sum, in order that the effort for the suffering might take place with greater generosity as well as more promptly."[7] But more on that later.[8] I have cited these texts to show the reasoning followed by the primitive church, which was still fervent and dripping with the blood of Christ and which strove to ensure that the poor would not have to travel through foreign lands. She did not confine them within certain borders through prohibitions on leaving, but provided for their basic needs so successfully that they were no longer compelled to leave. Therefore, my amazement could not have been greater: How could the emperor have been requested to obtain an apostolic letter from the pope stating that the poor are not allowed to beg outside of their native land? How could the pope have granted such a letter, unless both he and the emperor obliged in the strictest of ways each and every city to support the poor? This would have required that praetors be able to force citizens to provide the poor with appropriate food, clothing, and other necessities, just like they pay other taxes. We have touched on this matter before.[9]

---

[5] Cyprian, *Epistulae*, I, ep. 10. Ed. note: ep. II.2, 3. C. Bayard, ed., *Saint Cyprien, Correspondance: Texte établi par le Chanoine Bayard* (Paris: Les Belles Lettres, 1925), 5. The original letter spoke of a single poor person, not of a group.

[6] Cyprian, *Epistulae*, III, ep. 10. Ed. note: ep. XIV.2, 1. Bayard, *Saint Cyprien, Correspondance*, 40.

[7] Cyprian, *Epistulae*, ep. 24. Ed. note: ep. VII.2. Bayard, *Saint Cyprien, Correspondance*, 18.

[8] Ed. note: On the attitude of the early church toward the poor, see ch. 12, arg. 3, pp. 118–21.

[9] Ed. note: In ch. 4, arg. 2, pp. 30–32.

Such a law might—as I already said before—be neither just nor easily enforceable. But more on this later.[10]

Objections

The arguments on which the authors of the petitions relied, and which may have given them the feeling that they were striving for nothing but equity, could have been more or less the following. First, they might have reasoned that no province has an obligation toward the poor from outside its borders, and that each province rather has a duty toward its own poor only. For if this were not the case, the burden of the poor masses would be unevenly carried more by one province than by another.

But this reasoning is refuted in two steps. First, based on what has been said before,[11] we admit that no province is legally bound to take care of the poor of another province. For no one is obliged to be generous toward a beggar who is not suffering from a state of extreme necessity. Yet it does not immediately follow from this that a beggar can be kept within the borders of his land, as if he did not have the right, given everybody's basic liberty, of begging wherever he wants from the person he wants, and of trying to appeal with his supplications to the mercy of the person of his choice. Moreover, the richer the citizens of a province—because God has distributed the goods of fortune more lavishly among them—the more generous must be the alms to the poor of Christ, whatever their origin. Otherwise, God would not have provided for human life with much forethought, even though he is the Lord of all.

But perhaps someone might reply that we have in the first place, according to the order of charity, an obligation toward those to whom we are related by blood ties or another close connection, and to our fellow citizens rather than foreigners. This is what Paul taught to the

---

[10] Ed. note: In ch. 11, many reasons are given for why it is so difficult to enact a just law which prohibits begging.

[11] Ed. note: See ch. 4, arg. 3, pp. 32–34.

Galatians when he said, "As long as we have time, let us do good to all men, but especially to those who are of the household of the faith."[12]

However, we reply in the following way to this objection. First, Paul did not only admonish us to be benefactors toward the members of our own household, but to all men, whatever their nation or condition. The only thing he teaches is that when greater resources are not available, we should start with those nearer to us. A second response should, with regard to this topic, be more attentively noted. That someone has a stronger obligation toward his own kin than toward outsiders—which is the only thing Paul teaches—is certainly one thing, but that outsiders and foreigners should be deprived of their right to ask any human being for alms is something completely different, especially among Christians. That can never be licit. A city might perhaps have a right to keep foreigners out for as long as it finds itself in a situation of extreme poverty and famine and is unable to provide for itself on account of the extreme want it is suffering. Nevertheless, I would hardly be able to advise this for such times. Furthermore, since the calamity of famine would be assailing the kingdom in its entirety, everyone would have the right to seek nourishment wherever he can find it. It would then suffice to remind the people that he who cannot help everyone should prioritize helping his own.

The second argument used to justify the aforementioned petitions is that there could be people who might have enough goods to live from but still pretend to be poor when traveling to a different province. Indeed, through their fraud they take away alms which could have been allocated better to the local and truly legitimate poor. Moreover, they carry contagious diseases and plagues from one region into another. Other similar inconveniences are recorded in the previously mentioned petitions. I acknowledge the obvious truth that there exists no social rank or order among men in which there are not both good and bad men, honest and dishonest, as I will discuss more extensively further on.[13] Nevertheless, when a social rank and condition as a whole is licit, bad members of this rank have to be punished to prevent the

---

[12] Gal. 6:10.

[13] See ch. 9, cons. 5, pp. 71–74.

social rank from suffering injustice. Since the social condition of the poor, including of the poor foreigners and pilgrims, is considered licit among us, it should suffice that the false poor are punished when they are caught, as it happens in other social orders of men in accordance with law and custom. Therefore, it is not necessary to root out poor foreigners completely. This is especially because those who have provisions at home and move to a different place in order to feign being a beggar are so rare that no law is needed for them on account of their small number. There is also no need to fear that beggars, on account of their large number, would ever cause a great financial loss to a province or city. Regarding what they allege about the spreading of plagues, frequently it is not the foreigners who transmit such plagues. Rather, any crowd of poor people, wherever it may be and even if it consists of locals, tends to cause outbreaks of diseases and plagues.

No further argument comes to mind which anyone could raise with minimal credibility against foreigners and pilgrims who are legitimately poor.

6

The Pilgrims to Saint James

Directly appended to the previous article is the article concerning the pilgrims to Saint James. That is, "that they cannot hang around in a place longer than needed or deviate from the correct path for more than twelve miles." I do not want to waste too many words on this so that I may not seem to tarnish everything with my speech, but it will be enough to remind you of a few things.

Pilgrimage

First, since pilgrimage is an honorable and religious work, and certainly not the least among the works pertaining to divine worship, it is inappropriate to ordain anything in apparent hatred of pilgrimage because of this or that person who acts like a vagabond under a pilgrim's guise. This is especially true at a time when images, shrines, and venerations of the saints have such a bad reputation among those neoteric defilers and scorners of religion. Consider especially that pilgrims are foreigners who come to us from external regions, mostly for religious purposes. This means that we might give scandal to other kingdoms if we force pilgrims to walk like sheep on a prescribed and fully enclosed path. Even now, the barrenness of the route can hardly sustain such a large turnout of pilgrims, even with simple bread.

Nonetheless, pursuant to the right of hospitality and the right of religion, they should be refreshed in our midst more lavishly and with more generosity. Moreover, the interior of the kingdom also contains several sanctuaries, and to visit them is a religious activity as well. What if a desire to visit the court of Your Highness or some prominent cities in the kingdom would overtake some people? Would it not be uncivilized and almost inhumane to deny them the use of roads or alms? I would believe, beyond any doubt, that they would then be able to accuse us on account of violations against the law of nations, even if we had allowed them to determine the time of their return to their homeland. I believe the court only wanted to declare that those pretending to be pilgrims and staying for a long time at the court or elsewhere in the kingdom should be transferred to their own places of residence, following *Authenticum* "On the quaestor."[1] For they should already have been judged like vagabonds under those circumstances.

If gracious hospitality is due to pilgrims going to the thresholds of the apostle,[2] the visitors to the holy sites in Jerusalem deserve it far more because the mysteries of our salvation were carried out there. Truly, there the feet of Christ our Savior have stood, there his blood was shed, and his body buried. Because of that humiliation unto death on the cross, he received a name before which every knee shall bow.[3] God charged the famous city of Venice with the responsibility of ensuring that this religious duty, which is one of the most important, could be carried out. For it is the port through which the pilgrims going to the Holy Land pass and where they have to be refreshed with all kindness on their way back.

---

[1] Ed. note: Nov. 80, 3.

[2] Ed. note: i.e., Santiago de Compostela.

[3] Ed. note: Phil. 2:10.

Epilogue

These are the things which, so it seems, should be learned from the initial part of our disputation. I had set out to analyze what can be legitimately ordained by law with regard to the poor and what would be in no way licit. I am not sure whether I succeeded, but it was merely my intention to demonstrate that the only distinction we must make among the poor is based on whether they are legitimate or whether they are false and pretending to be poor. It is not permissible by any right to further distinguish between groups of natives and residents on the one side, and aliens and foreigners on the other. As long as they are legitimate, foreigners and pilgrims have the right to beg indiscriminately. Nevertheless, the correct order of charity demands that, all things being equal, those who cannot give to everyone should first confer alms to their fellow countrymen, as long as all others are not deprived of their right to beg. Those who falsely pretend to be poor, however, whether citizens or foreigners, should be banished as idle men.

7

THE FINAL END OF THE PLAN FOR THE POOR

The second part of this deliberation discusses the plan and method[1] we should follow in instituting and enforcing legitimate policies for the poor, in order to ensure that this is done in a more optimal way that comes closer to the ideals of the Christian religion.

Six Articles

Above we summarized in six articles the proposal circulating on the treatment of the poor.[2] The first article states that no one can beg before his poverty has been established through lawful examination. The second, that no one can beg outside of his native land. The third, that no one is allowed to beg without written permission. The fourth, that written permissions are only granted to those who have first made their confession in the sacrament. The fifth concerns the pilgrims to Saint James. The sixth and most famous article of all states that the poor should not be allowed to beg by going from door to door through

---

[1] *rationem modumque.*

[2] Ed. note: See ch. 2, pp. 13–14. Please note the discrepancy in the description of the sixth article.

Deliberation on the Cause of the Poor

the streets. I believe enough has already been said about the second[3] and the fifth[4] articles, making it unnecessary to discuss them again. The first article, however, which pertains to an examination, has the authority of law, as is obvious from the third chapter.[5] However, what is called into question is how exactly such an examination should be put into practice. For this reason, we inevitably have to add the third[6] and fourth[7] articles to our analysis. The last place is reserved for the sixth article.[8]

The Final End of the Plan

First of all, we should determine the end to which the entire plan and duty toward the poor is aimed. This is what Aristotle advises frequently. For he says in the seventh book of his *Nicomachean Ethics* that in our planning as in our every action, the end comes before everything else.[9] The end functions in every prudent and provident undertaking like the target of an archer at which he aims his arrow.[10] Therefore he concludes that the means should be judged according to the end.[11] Cicero states in his work *On Invention* with more clarity that the end

---

[3] Ed. note: The second article concerns foreign beggars and is discussed in chs. 4 and 5.

[4] Ed. note: The fifth article about the pilgrims to Santiago is discussed in ch. 6.

[5] Ed. note: See ch. 3, pp. 24–25. For more on the first article, see ch. 10.

[6] Ed. note: The written permission required by the third article is alluded to throughout the work. However, especially relevant are chs. 9 and 10 (particularly ch. 9, p. 101).

[7] Ed. note: The fourth article is discussed explicitly in ch. 10, pp. 85–87.

[8] Ed. note: The sixth article is discussed in ch. 11.

[9] Aristotle, *Nicomachean Ethics* VII. Ed. note: VII.11 (1152b), cf. VI.9 (1142b).

[10] Ed. note: Aristotle, *Nicomachean Ethics* I.2 (1094a).

[11] Ed. note: Aristotle, *Nicomachean Ethics* V.2 (1130b).

of each duty should be put first.¹² In our case, it should be avoided above all that those petitions, regulations, and plans for the poor would ultimately arise from the weariness and nausea which beggars tend to cause through their appearance and shamelessness among certain thin-skinned people of our time. The Wisest and Most Equitable Royal Senate is, of course, only moved by sacred intention and evangelic zeal, allowing it to carefully respond to what is so boldly asked.

The persons that I have known who carry out this office and duty are driven by mercy and pious intention to take better care of the legitimate poor and those who are dying from starvation. But nevertheless, the wording of these constitutions certainly cannot prevent distrustful people from suspecting that at least some among the initial authors—I do not want to put everyone under suspicion—devised such severe constitutions in order to banish from their midst the commotion and irritation caused by beggars rather than to distribute the alms more correctly. What if Saint Ambrose or definitely Saint Chrysostom heard that that miserable class, or mass of the poor, was being encircled by so many laws! For only if they have been diligently examined, have confessed their sins, have a handwritten document, are within the limits of their native land, and finally confined at home do they at last receive mere pennies which hardly allow them to live. Truly, the saints would have thought that these laws were only laid down out of hatred for a class that actually deserves pity. And if we respond that these laws were not devised out of hatred, they would still not be demonstrative of the heart and disposition with which Christ, the Father of the Poor, wanted us to act toward his children. How, Most Renowned Prince, do you think we will keep the name of the miserable poor from becoming hateful to Christians or being held in contempt and mockery? Clearly on that awe-inspiring day, those who despise that name shall, as the Book of Wisdom says, be "terrified with horrible fear, and amazed at the suddenness of their unexpected salvation."¹³ Undoubtedly, they will confess when they see those so dissimilar fortunes and positions

---

12 Ed. note: Cicero, *De inventione* 1.5; but see *De officiis* I.2–3, 7.

13 Ed. note: Wis. 5:2. The verse speaks of the amazement of the condemned at the salvation of the just.

of the rich and of the poor switch places. "Then they shall groan from anguish, repenting and lamenting among themselves: Those are the ones whom we once held in derision, and for a parable of reproach. We fools esteemed their life madness, and their end without honor. Behold, how they are numbered among the children of God, and their lot is among the saints."[14] In fact, even if the name of the poor were not honorable on the basis of any other right or merit, it should still be most commendable for Christians because Christ our Savior—whom we should believe chose only the best rank among mortals—chose the condition of a poor man. Add to that that the rich do not meet with his approval anywhere in Sacred Scripture, while on the other hand the whole Gospel is completely filled with favors, privileges, and recommendations for the poor.

Not that the condition and rank of princes and of others who are established in some position of dignity and power are not greatly approved by the Gospel. For since all power is from the Lord God (as Paul taught[15]), it is most just for them to be held in the highest honor and esteem. But nevertheless, nowhere did Christ consider the abundance of wealth and the flow of material goods stemming from fortune worthy of honor like he did poverty. And that is to still overlook the kingly psalmist who foretold everywhere that Christ would come to "bring justice to the poor of the people and to save the sons of the poor."[16] And neither shall he allow "the patience of the poor to perish," but he shall "hear their desire."[17] Christ himself, our Savior, began his Sermon on the Mount by quelling the foolish, swollen arrogance of those who found happiness in their numerous possessions and their fortune. For he said, "Blessed are the poor in spirit, for theirs is the kingdom of heaven."[18] But he does not only call those "poor in spirit" who have freely professed their poverty through a religious vow, but

---

[14] Ed. note: Wis. 5:3–5.

[15] Rom. 13:1.

[16] Ps. 71:4.

[17] Ps. 9:38.

[18] Ed. note: Matt. 5:3.

also all of those who bear their need and mendicancy with a calm mind. And he chose from among the common poor people those whom he would appoint as princes of the world and promulgators of the law. And I hope that I will not be loathed when recounting all relevant passages, but Christ never compared the poor with the rich except to honor the poor. In the early church the poor were held in great esteem by the apostles who were appointed by Christ, as is recorded by Saint James: "Should a man come into our assembly, wearing a golden ring and in shining attire; and should a poor man come as well, wearing mean attire, we should not prefer to give up our seat to the rich man rather than to the poor."[19] "Otherwise," he said, "we would be discriminating between persons."[20] For the apostles taught Christians that we should assess and judge persons solely on the merit of their virtue, excluding those who are in high office.[21] For nothing else will be taken into consideration when the comedy of this world comes to an end, when the masks which we see now are taken off, and when the truth of our merits is revealed. How could we extol the fate of the poor more sublimely? Since God, according to the testimony of David,[22] has no need of our goods, he has devised an amazing technique to require the assistance of the rich. For it was not enough for him to say, "What you did for one of the least of these brothers of mine, you did for me and I shall recompense you,"[23] although he would have commended almsgiving already eminently with this statement alone. Rather he said, "What you did for one of the least of these brothers of mine, you did to me. For I was the hungry person you fed, the naked person

---

[19] James 2:2–4. Ed. note: Only James 2:2 is quoted literally.

[20] James 2:9. Ed. note: Soto's original here reads: *acceptores essemus personarum*.

[21] Ed. note: The reading in the Spanish text of 1545 is clearer: "*viniere algún rico—entiende que no sean hombres de dignidad y governación—y viniere también un pobre*" (Christians should not show preference to rich people when giving up their seat, except if they are dignitaries or people in high office). Soto, *Relecciones y opúsculos*, II-2, 265.

[22] Ed. note: cf. Ps. 49:8–13.

[23] Matt. 25:40.

you clothed, and the stranger you received."[24] And this is not only the case in this world in which the Divine Sublimity deigned to take on the character of a poor man, but will also be true on that renowned day of his when he will plainly demonstrate the magnificence of his unfathomable majesty to all the ranks of heaven, earth, and hell. On that day he will not disdain to admit that he has spent time among us as a poor person and a beggar. Please excuse me, Prince abounding in all the ornaments of the virtues, for having allowed myself such a long digression in order to honor the name of the poor. I thought it would greatly serve the present purpose.

Luis Vives[25]

For there are those who express themselves publicly on the subject of poor relief[26] and immediately get off to an inauspicious start by slandering, namely, by depicting with much drama and rhetoric the immodesty, impudence, rapaciousness, and ingratitude of poor people, as well as their skill in feigning illnesses.[27] By recounting their evil deeds, they incite hatred toward this miserable class.

They add that they "had not said these things about everyone without exception, but in general."[28] But since they only touched upon the behavior of certain individuals, the class itself should still remain highly commended to Christians. No type of craftsmen, no rank of citizens, no family, and no ecclesiastical grade or institution may be blamed or debased in its totality on account of the crimes of individuals, so

---

[24] Matt. 25:35.

[25] Ed. note: This critique of the opinions of Vives cannot be found in the edition of 1545.

[26] Ed. note: Juan Luis Vives, *De subventione pauperum, sive de humanis necessitatibus libri II* (Bruges: Hubert de Croock, 1526). Cf. Vives, *De subventione pauperum sive de humanis necessitatibus, libri II*, ed. C. Matheeussen, C. Fantazzi, J. De Landtsheer, vol. 4 of *Selected Works of Juan Luis Vives*, ed. C. Fantazzi (Leiden: Brill, 2002).

[27] Ed. note: Vives, *De subventione pauperum* I.5, 5–6 (Brill ed., 30–33).

[28] Ed. note: Vives, *De subventione pauperum* I.5, 7 (Brill ed., 32–33).

how much less with poor people whom Christ wanted us to consider as his substitutes.

They claim to express reproach of wicked beggars because they want to prove that a benefaction should only be handed out to those who are worthy, and also that the poor should show gratitude. This is according to those ancient verses:[29] "He receives a benefit through his gift if he gives something to someone who is worthy of it."[30] And that of Ennius: "I consider badly oriented good deeds to be bad deeds."[31] But that doctrine is not supported by any testimonies except from pagans who had not yet heard the reasons for almsgiving from the mouth of Christ, the Patron of the Poor. For how much gratitude could you want from a poor person to whom you have granted a miserable coin? Or what does it matter to you that a poor person is ungrateful, if "what you did to one of Christ's little ones, you did to him,"[32] who even promised a reward for a drink of cold water?[33] Surely he did not want us to be so anxiously concerned about the gratitude of beggars, preaching that "when you make lunch or dinner, do not invite your friends, nor your brothers, nor your relatives, nor your rich neighbors, lest they invite you back and repay you. Rather, when you give a banquet, invite the poor, and the feeble, and the lame, and the blind. And you will be blessed, because they do not have the means to repay you, but you will be repaid at the resurrection of the just."[34] And when he said, "When you give alms, do not let your left hand know what your

---

[29] Ed. note: These verses were cited in Vives, *De subventione pauperum* I.5, 1 (Brill ed., 26–27).

[30] Ed. note: Publilius Syrus, *Sententiae*: "*Beneficium dando accepit, digno qui dedit.*"

[31] Ed. note: Ennius, as quoted by Cicero in *De officiis* II.18, 62: "*Bene facta, male locata, male facta arbitror.*"

[32] Ed. note: Matt. 25:40 (also cited above).

[33] Ed. note: Matt. 10:42.

[34] Ed. note: Luke 14:12–14.

Deliberation on the Cause of the Poor

right hand is doing."[35] Nicholas[36] and the most holy fathers of his kind have always understood this to mean that, if possible, even the poor person should be kept ignorant of the source of the alms he receives, so that his act of gratitude may not degrade the good grace and merit of the giver. However, we have departed from our topic, for we were saying that it should be absolutely avoided that these regulations render the name of the poor odious or less deserving in any way.[37]

And it would not be good if the aim and goal of this undertaking would be to lighten the burden of almsgiving borne by the republic by expelling the vagabonds. It was not just for that reason alone that so much effort had to be invested, so many officials appointed and armed with so many laws. For there are those in the republic who, by means of less licit contracts and even fraud and deceit, secretly steal the property of others and to a far greater degree than the vagabonds. But none of these machinations are aimed at them.

I would like to add that the following logic should be followed: all alms which are taken away from the vagabonds should be integrally added to the amount received by the legitimate poor, and the poor people, cleansed of vagabonds, should be held in higher esteem and be showered with greater alms. Otherwise by expelling the vagabonds, the rich will incur damage rather than receive benefit.

As a matter of fact, as great as the amount of almsgiving they perform may be, they are still not fulfilling the just amount of alms they are bound to give. If the only intention of the republic in these constitutions is to reduce the practice of almsgiving, then clearly it is much better for the citizens whom mercy cannot convince to be more lenient toward the poor to be defeated by the impudence of legitimate beggars and even deceived by the cunningness of the false poor.

Neither does the intention to amend the moral character of the poor suffice to justify this undertaking. For surely if the poor had the opportunity, perhaps they would be able to discover many faults in us

---

[35] Ed. note: Matt. 6:3.

[36] Ed. note: Nicholas of Myra, renowned for his generosity.

[37] Ed. note: The is the end of Soto's critique of the opinions of Vives, an addition not included in the edition of 1545.

which they could correct. Besides, as I will explain more extensively below,[38] it would be good if the secular and ecclesiastical authorities responsible for the rich would also take up the responsibility of caring for the poor. Nevertheless, I would not object if the procurators of the poor with regard to their temporal condition would, basically in the course of doing something else, also occupy themselves with their moral character.

The Aim of the Constitutions on the Poor

Therefore, the aim and goal of the offices which are being instituted for the sake of the poor should be that the truly poor may be better cared for by means of almsgiving. More precisely, that they may receive greater assistance regarding their temporal needs, and that there should not only be no decrease in the alms, but rather that following this plan, there should be an increase. This is the end to which all regulations should be meticulously directed, and we have to choose and carry out whatever is most conducive to the attainment of this goal.

---

[38] Ed. note: See ch. 9 and ch. 12, particularly pp. 68–69 and 123–24.

8

THE OBLIGATION BY WHICH CHRISTIANS ARE BOUND TO GIVE ALMS

Now that we have envisaged the aim of our undertaking, it is worthwhile to warn the rich. For they should know that the alms which they confer to the aid of the needy are not really so much paid out by them from their *own* possessions as the common people might have made them to believe. Alms are, after all, owed to the poor with a far stronger obligation than they estimate. For God truly provides all things and not only concerns himself with bringing forth grass for the cattle,[1] but also with decorating both the grass itself, which exists today and is thrown into the oven tomorrow, as well as the lilies in the field, clothing them both with more beauty than even Solomon in all his glory was ever clothed.[2] Therefore, he could never have been so neglectful of the human race as to intentionally leave the needy so deprived of aid among men of great wealth, which is how we find them now among Christians. The reason why he made sure that the rich have an abundance of goods was not to inundate them with superfluous goods, but to make sure that those superfluous goods flow to the poor and the needy. In rare cases, he also permitted some people to get rich to prepare their destruction. He did not arrange things this way without a profound intention, but rather wanted to bring the human

---

[1] Ed. note: Ps. 104:14.
[2] Ed. note: cf. Matt. 6:28–30; Luke 12:27–28.

race together with a closer tie and with a sort of bond of charity that they might be like parts of a single body. The reason why, by nature, all parts of the body hold one another so dear is that each part needs the help of another part. God wanted men to recognize that both the rich and the poor have the same Lord and Father, since he had appointed the rich as stewards over the poor that they might distribute their wealth among them. By the same token in the natural realm, God wanted, by nature, the earth to be subject to heavenly motions so that it might take strength from the power distributed by those celestial motions.[3] That is why theologians put forward this most powerful argument in order to testify for the one God: that all the parts of the universe hold each other in such a tight embrace of friendship that, had they not been of the same origin, there would never have been such brotherly affection between them. Therefore, the apostle John who is, according to Christ, the greatest teacher of love, says with great certitude that "he who possesses worldly wealth and sees his brother in need, but closes his heart to him, can by no means be in charity."[4]

From this Saint Thomas concluded wisely, first of all, that alms have to be given to those who are in extreme need as a matter of precept.[5] This is what Ambrose reminded us of when he said, "Feed him who is dying of hunger; if you have not fed him, you have killed him."[6] But importantly the holy doctor added, second, that anyone who possesses something in greater quantity than is required by the standards of his own class is obliged to give alms. The conclusion is evident. For if we are obliged according to the gospel to love our neighbor as ourselves,[7] and if "he who closes his heart to his neighbor in need does not love

---

[3] Ed. note: On Soto's natural philosophy, which is known to have inspired Galileo Galilei, see W. A. Wallace, "Domingo de Soto's 'Laws' of Motion: Text and Context," in *Texts and Contexts in Ancient and Medieval Science*, ed. E. Sylla and M. R. McVaugh (Leiden: Brill, 1997), 271–304.

[4] 1 John 3:17.

[5] Thomas Aquinas, *Summa theologiae* II-2, q. 32, a. 5.

[6] Ed. note: Dec. Grat. Dist.86 c.21.

[7] Ed. note: Matt. 22:39; Mark 12:31; Luke 10:27; John 13:34–35; Gal. 5:14; cf. Lev. 19:18.

The Obligation to Give Alms

his brother," as the apostle testified, "because he is not in charity," then that kind of man is violating the law. Furthermore, he sins mortally because his charity is lost through that single sin. Neither can anyone invoke the fact that John might have talked about a brother in extreme necessity as an excuse to turn his back on his obligation. For if he had only meant that kind of necessity, namely, extreme necessity, he would not have added, "if he possesses worldly wealth."[8] For even he who does not possess worldly wealth, that is, an abundance of goods, is bound to help those who find themselves in such extreme necessity to the best of his ability. Therefore, rich men are sometimes bound by precept to give alms even outside of cases of extreme necessity. This is corroborated by additional divine testimony which can be found in Luke.[9] There, Christ rebuked certain people because they bore no fruit of virtue, and should therefore, like a barren tree, be cut down and thrown into the fire. When some of them wanted to know what the best way would be to protect themselves from this danger, he replied that "he who has two tunics should give one to him who has none, and he who has food should do likewise."[10] Notice that no mention of extreme necessity is made here. However, to make sure that everyone protects himself from the fire of hell (which nobody will be thrown into unless he has committed a mortal sin), every person is ordered to share his goods with the poor. A large amount of wealth is not required. After all he said, "He who has two tunics should give one to him who has none." Indeed, it is thought that one tunic is enough for life, and everyone who has more is admonished to pass it on to the needy. But the scholastic theologians did not want to appear exceedingly terrifying to the rich, and therefore devised many conditions which have to be fulfilled before they would oblige men to give alms under pain of mortal sin. Namely, the rich have to have a surplus and the poor have to be in serious need, as well as other similar conditions.

---

[8] 1 John 3:17.

[9] Luke 3:7–11. Ed. note: The person uttering these words of rebuke is not Christ but John the Baptist.

[10] Luke 3:10–11.

Deliberation on the Cause of the Poor

It is not my intention now to propose a narrower and, as they say, more scrupulous definition because I am not discussing this subject scholastically. Yet at any rate when I read the holy fathers attentively, I do not believe that they required such a grave need among the poor, or among the rich such large abundance beyond what suits their class, before they demanded alms to be given under pain of mortal sin. Perhaps they hardly believed that there could be a man who, not being poor himself, does not possess at least something which he has to give away. If one thousand are not superfluous to someone, perhaps he still has an excess of one hundred, and if not of one hundred, then at least of ten. In the end, who would have to injure his house to come to the aid of the poor in one way or another? That's why Ambrose said in his commentary on Luke, included in the canon *In singulis*, "The use of mercy is common to all, and therefore the precept commonly obliges as well. A soldier is not exempted; neither is a farmer, nor a city dweller. The rich and poor are all commonly admonished to give to those who do not have. For mercy fulfills the virtues, and is therefore a form of perfect virtue recommended to everyone."[11] But if we consider the wants of the poor and calamities by which they are struck to be insignificant, I can only fear vehemently what will happen on the day of judgment when we will know with certainty that those should have been the situations in which we were supposed to help them. From here stems that type of language used by the holy fathers in which they call the greed and harshness of the rich toward the poor nothing less than theft and robbery. The following words of Jerome are in the canon *Hospitalem*: "If it is proven that someone keeps more for himself than he needs, he is convicted of stealing the goods of others."[12] Ambrose added even harsher words in his commentary on Luke when he explained the parable of the rich man who pondered how he could avoid giving away his crops and how to store them for himself, and then suddenly died.[13] The words of Ambrose can be found in the canon *Sicut hi*, in which he asks the greedy rich

---

[11] Dec. Grat. Dist.86 c.19.

[12] Dec. Grat. Dist.42 c.1*pr*.

[13] Ed. note: Luke 12:16–21.

man why he had kept for himself what he should have given away to the poor and receives the following reply: "What injustice is done, if, without seizing the goods of other people, I diligently preserve my own?" To which Ambrose replies with these words:

> O shameless speaker! What is it that you call 'your own'? What is it, and from which hiding place did you bring it with you into this world? No one should call his own what is common to all. Anything beyond what is needed to meet one's expenses is obtained through violence. Or is God unfair, and did he therefore distribute the means of life unevenly among us, letting you be affluent and abounding in wealth, but allowing others to lack it and to be in need? Rather, the real reason is that God wanted to grant you the experience of his favor, and to crown others through the virtue of patience.[14]

Wise and pious as they were, the fathers considered God to have conferred these goods upon the human race in its entirety. These goods were later divided by the law of nations, but without preventing that in situations of necessity, the common use of all goods would still be available to all. Should we be at all surprised if the saints have spoken in that way, considering the words uttered by the divine mouth in Isaiah: "the plunder of the poor is in your houses,"[15] which, if Chrysostom in his second sermon on Lazarus[16] is to be believed, have to be interpreted as referring to the alms of the poor which are withheld from them by the rich? He meant that the rich have an abundance of what Isaiah mentioned with reproach in the same passage, namely, their ornaments such as their "little moons, collars, necklaces, armlets, headbands,"[17] and the like, and that they can only acquire this abundance by stealing from the poor. But there are things that, even more

---

[14] Dec. Grat. Dist.47 c.8.

[15] Isa. 3:14.

[16] Chrysostom, *De Lazaro concio secunda* 4 (PG 48:987–88).

[17] Isa. 3:18–19.

than the aforementioned, vehemently trouble me with regard to this issue, and not only me but Augustine as well.

The first is this saying of the Lord: "You cannot serve God and mammon."[18] And what does it mean except that you cannot at the same time yield to your desire for riches and have that merciful concern for the poor which the Lord ordered you to have in large quantities? The second is the fact which that holiest and wisest father greatly marveled at in his interpretation of the same passage:[19]

> For even though there are so many sins, crimes, and shameful acts because of which men have to be condemned for eternity, nevertheless, in the Gospel, no mention is made of something that can be held against them on the Day of the Lord in order to bring about their eternal damnation, except for: "I was hungry, and you did not give me anything to eat; I was thirsty, and you did not give me anything to drink; I was naked, and you did not cover me; finally, I was a stranger, and you did not receive me."[20]

So much for Augustine.

The truth is therefore completely obvious, unless we have been blinded by the vilest greed and unless we react to the divine word in the manner of vipers: the precept of almsgiving has a much wider scope and applies in many more cases than harsh men have falsely believed. Otherwise, how could the conviction on that day for neglecting the duty of mercy apply to all men in general? But this is not the right place, and it is not my present intention, to completely analyze the matter. The following should suffice, if I may only add this last word: Assume that God is the Father of all, both of the rich and of the poor, and that he has, like the head of a family, the responsibility to look after and provide for everyone. It necessarily follows from this either that God has had little foresight because he has left the indigent and the

---

[18] Ed. note: Matt. 6:24; Luke 16:13.

[19] Augustine, *Sermo* LX.9–11 (PL 38:406–8).

[20] Ed. note: cf. Matt. 25:42–43.

beggars helpless, or that the rich have to be rebuked for their perfidy and inhumanity. For God entrusted the poor to their care and placed them under their authority, but they claim for themselves the goods which were put into their care, deny that they were handed over, and do not keep the faith.

9

THE EXAMINATION OF THE POVERTY OF THE BEGGARS

Now that we have been instructed by the explanation of these foundations, we can finally move on to the first article which treats of the examination of the poor.[1] Although the examination itself is required by law, the question of how rigorously it should be executed remains subject to deliberation.

Two Criteria to Be Examined

Such articles designate the two things which we have to examine in the poor. The first is their poverty and indigence, whether they are real or false poor. The second is their morals and way of life. The first criterion is described in the third article, the second in the fourth article. Regarding the first criterion, it is equitable and worthwhile to remove feigned and pretending beggars from our midst. This has been abundantly demonstrated in the first conclusion.[2]

Consideration I

We should first of all take into consideration that it is one thing for men to be merciful toward the miserable and another thing for them

---

[1] Ed. note: The content of each article is summarized in ch. 2, pp. 13–14.

[2] Ed. note: See ch. 3 in its entirety.

to exercise justice toward the depraved and unrighteous. God commanded all men to be merciful but entrusted the punishment of wrongdoers to a few servants of justice. According to the testimony of Paul, they "bear the sword" so that they may be "avengers who bring wrath to the wrongdoers."[3] For this reason we have to ask ourselves whether it would not be good if those same officials who are responsible for the administration of justice to the other classes of citizens, the improvement of their behavior, and the punishment of their sins would also seek out vagabonds, sanction them, and take care to repress them. Alternatively, senators and the governors of the cities[4] could also round up the beggars once a week or once a month and punish the ones whom they can prove to be able-bodied. They may either condemn them to work and labor or banish them from the city. But to appoint more praetors as executors aimed at the poor rather than the rich—with no task other than to seek out the poor, summon them, assess them, and drive them out—that is something which someone might judge to arise not so much from mercy for the genuine poor as from hatred toward the class of the poor in its entirety. This is especially the case since the crimes of the rich are not investigated so actively by the praetors. Rather, they consider their duty fulfilled if they correct those who are brought before them in accordance with the law. It is therefore not necessary to track down the poor more assiduously.

Consideration 2

Now we should consider that that miserable, ignoble, and powerless group of men do not have the capacity to defend their own cause. For as we quoted shortly before from Ecclesiasticus, "The rich man was the wrongdoer, yet continues to rage, but the poor man was wronged and will remain silent."[5] And Ecclesiastes says, "The wisdom of a poor man is despised, and his words are not heard."[6] Consequently, a rich

---

[3] Rom. 13:4.

[4] *rectores urbium.*

[5] Ed. note: Ecclesiasticus 13:3.

[6] Eccl. 9:16.

man accused of some crime or asked to pay an outstanding debt can protect himself with a lawsuit, with weapons, or through some other means. But a beggar, even if he is falsely accused, has no shield with which to protect himself. Inevitably, he has to endure the injustice. Add to that the fact that if you unjustly take away part of a rich man's possessions, he still retains a portion to live from, but if you prevent a very hard-hit beggar from begging, you kill that miserable person. That is why God declares himself in so many places to be the Father of the orphans, the widows, and the poor.[7] For the same reason, the church fathers imposed the large responsibility to take care of the poor on the prelates. Citing all the testimonies for the latter would be an immense work. All of this of course is because a poor man has no defense from the powerful. Since that class of miserable people is steeped in envy and rivalries, you can hardly find a truthful testimony when you inquire about the poverty of one of them. Some of them falsely accuse others; every one of them preoccupies himself with fraud in order to obtain what is confiscated from others.

Superintendents of the Poor

If people are assigned to execute such inquiries and examinations, it is really necessary given all the previous reasons that they are not of just any rank and reputation, but of a particular kind of men that is more inclined toward the leniency of mercy than toward the severity of justice and quicker to support the poor than to act to their detriment. For if the official executors are appointed from among the common people,[8] they might conceal under their mantle the poverty which they have to look for in others, and easily sell justice for a price. Consequently, they would accuse those unable to offer them anything of being perfectly able-bodied.

---

[7] Ed. note: On *personae miserabiles*, see Thomas Duve, *Sonderrecht in der Frühen Neuzeit. Studien zum* ius singulare *und den* privilegia miserabilium personarum, senum *und* indorum *in Alter und Neuer Welt* (Frankfurt am Main: Klostermann, 2008).

[8] *plebs*.

Consideration 3

With regard to this issue we should not pass over the fact that it is not necessary to be sick in order to qualify as legitimately poor. For it is enough to be advanced in age, or weak, or held back by any other impediment that inhibits one from enduring enough work to sufficiently provide for oneself and one's family. The same is written with foresight in the law *On able-bodied beggars* in Justinian's Code.[9] Its title is not *On healthy beggars* but *On able-bodied beggars*. Therefore, it is not the man who is healthy who should be immediately prohibited from begging, but he who is able-bodied.[10] Neither does the law which they call *Ordenamiento* pass over it in silence.[11] For it says that if there are men who can be declared able-bodied on the basis of their manifest appearance, they should be sentenced to work and labor. Therefore when their appearance and face show that they are not able-bodied, the law does not demand further checks or inquiries.

A Lesson

Hence, we should take the following lesson to heart: that in case of doubt when dealing with poor people, it is better to pronounce in favor of their poverty than to make a decision against them.[12]

For letting twenty wicked vagabonds through in order to avoid the exclusion from the city of four legitimately poor people is much less wicked and troublesome than withholding the right to beg from four people who are entitled to it in order to expel twenty able-bodied beggars. Following this reasoning, the head of the household wisely restrained the excessive zeal of his servants who were rushing to root

---

[9] Cod. 11.26.

[10] Ed. note: A distinction is made between a "healthy" (*sanus*) and an "able-bodied" (*validus*) beggar. Soto defines the term "able-bodied" in ch. 3, p. 24.

[11] *Lex illa quam appellant ordinamenti*. Ed. note: Nueva Recopilación 8.11.1–2.

[12] Ed. note: When deciding whether a beggar is truly poor or feigning his poverty.

up the tares, as can be found in Matthew, "lest in gathering the tares, they might also root up the wheat with them."[13]

Consideration 4

Directly linked to what was said previously is the fact that there are many who can, from time to time, bear work and labor, but not continually or too frequently. Someone might be able to handle working some days of the month or week, but not an entire month or week. Another might be able to work half a day, but not the whole day, and it would be the greatest possible nuisance for such a miserable man to have to go to the judges every time his strength fails him. In addition, there are those who, even though they are able-bodied, nevertheless have the right to beg: consider those who cannot find work or employers willing to hire them. If they do not find work in their own homeland, they can go anywhere they want to look for it.

For this reason, every city of the kingdom is certainly obliged either to support natives and foreigners or to allow them to beg, as long as the city has not assigned work to them or employers for whom they can work. Keeping the government of the kingdom in mind, those who cannot sustain themselves in one city should be received with kindness in another. Pursuant to this rule, the day laborers in the Gospel who were charged with idleness were rightly excused when they said, "because nobody has hired us."[14]

Consideration 5

To the aforementioned group of the unemployable also belong quite a few persons born of noble blood who are not strong enough to work with their hands and are too ashamed to beg. What I mean is that they are incapable of learning crafts and perhaps even of conducting business. They are under no obligation to lower themselves to vile servitude but have the right to receive a small handout from anyone, and one larger than those of lower class are entitled to.

---

[13] Matt. 13:29.

[14] Ed. note: Matt. 20:7.

Following the rigor of the law, we can grant all this. However, if we would regarding this topic consult the early fathers, who are like foundation stones laid by God under his church, we would have to say something very different about this examination of the poor. For the strongest argument supporting the inquisition of the poor is derived from the fact that there are many who destroy the republic through their fraudulent behavior. They devise many tricks by which they feign and pretend illness, injury, mutilation, and defects. There exists no greater deceit than that in a republic. But I nevertheless refer those making this argument to that great patron of the poor, Chrysostom, who made many statements in opposition to the abovementioned opinion, both in his thirty-seventh homily and in other works.[15] I pray and beseech everyone not to grow tired of hearing what he said.

After aggressively asking the rich why they do not use their garments, which the moth gnaws at and which the worm consumes, to clothe the naked,[16] he presented the following response of the rich: "The poor feign trembling and sickness." Greatest Prince, consider how the rich used these excuses for their avarice and threw these insults at the poor, even at the time of Chrysostom. Yet listen to the words with which Chrysostom railed against those who uttered such things. For he said,

> Do you not fear that, because of what you say, a thunderbolt could be set alight in heaven and be brought down upon you? Bear with me, for I am bursting with indignation! You are fat and swollen in the belly, you pull out a drink until late evening, and warm yourself with soft bedspreads, but you do not consider it appropriate for you to pay compensation? Although you yourself use the gifts of God immoderately (for wine is not there to intoxicate ourselves, and food was not created to gorge ourselves on it, and no nourishment to make our stomachs burst), you demand from a miserable poor

---

[15] Ed. note: Chrysostom, *In epistulam primam ad Corinthios Homilia* 21 (PG 61:169–80).

[16] Ed. note: The imagery of the moth and the worm stems from the Bible. We find it in Isa. 51:8 and Matt. 6:19, among other places.

person, who is of no better disposition than a dead man, that he give you some special reasons? Clearly, you do not fear Christ's horrifying and terrible tribunal.

After all, if he is pretending, he is pretending out of necessity and want. He acts like this because of your harshness and inhumanity, which is not moved to mercy by the pleas of such persons. For who is so miserable and wretched that he would, without suffering a pressing need, willingly disfigure and bewail himself, and suffer such severe punishment, all for a single piece of bread? Their fakery heralds your inhumanity. Even though he supplicates and beseeches, utters words of sadness, groans, weeps, and walks around the whole day, he does not find the nourishment he needs. Perhaps that is why he devised this trick, which does not bring as much disgrace and rebuke upon him as it does upon you. For anyone who falls in such great necessity deserves to find mercy. We, by contrast, are worthy of innumerable punishments for forcing the poor to endure such suffering. For if we would have given in more easily, they would never have chosen to be subjected to such things. And what should I say about nakedness and trembling? For I call it even more horrifying that certain people are forced to blind their children of immature age in order to overcome our insensible harshness. When they have the ability to see and wander around naked, they are not able to convince those who lack pity with only their young age and misery. They therefore add an even worse tragedy to these numerous evils in order to take away their hunger, because they believe that it is more bearable to be deprived of this common light and to go without that brilliance granted to everyone than to have a continuous fight with hunger and suffer a miserable death. Since you have not learned to pity poverty, but rejoice in their misfortunes, the poor satisfy your excessive desire and kindle a fiercer flame in hell, both for themselves and for you.[17]

---

[17] Ed. note: Chrysostom, *In epistulam primam ad Corinthios Homilia* 21.5 (PG 61:176–77).

Not with less Christian spirit than literary elegance were these words and others of the same emphasis thundered by Chrysostom against those who cruelly condemn the poor for sinning unnaturally against their own persons by ruining their bodies.

For those who are not moved by their supplications do not consider their own role, and therefore do not notice that their own inhumanity and savageness are responsible for the fact that the poor use these tragic tricks against them. If the rich would actually help the poor properly, the poor would, thanks to their wealth, never suffer those wants and wounds. But the poor are unable to obtain even a meager gift unless they contrive such tragedies. In all of this I am not contending, my splendid lord, that the vagabonds and the deceivers should not be reformed, but that others from every class or condition should also be reformed in a similar way. For there are persons among workmen, lawyers, scribes, clerics, friars, and magnates and even prelates, people of every class and rank who are so weak, criminal, and disgraceful that they are unworthy of the bread they eat.[18] But not so many investigators and executors turn their attention to them. For sins[19] should be purged with a sieve, but not a hair sieve. And as the *Decretum* says, "If all sins were punished in this world, there would be no place for divine judgment."[20]

Consideration 6

I do not intend to stigmatize any class of men or to dishonor anyone. But I can, without injustice, present what is obvious and manifestly true for the entire human race. For how many workmen or public servants are there in the republic who by fraud steal many more possessions than that entire crowd of able-bodied beggars, and thereupon squander them with displays of luxury and splendor? Yet men are able to tolerate their fraud and robberies with an even mind. But there is no way to

---

[18] Ed. note: Gen. 3:19.

[19] *crimina*. Ed. note: We have followed the reading of the Spanish text: "sins" (*peccados*).

[20] Dec. Grat. C.6 q.1 c.7.

convince those same men to tolerate a false pauper who is depriving someone of a miserable little coin by means of clever tricks, namely, by dragging his nudity, trembling, hunger, and infirmity around with him. On the contrary, they proclaim that such paupers should first be deprived of all light before receiving help. Was there ever a man who experienced any kind of damage to his abundant possessions on account of that deceitful crowd of pseudo-paupers? I will not mention those who acquire the property of someone else by means of less admissible contracts and business activities. Some individuals have amassed more possessions of unjust mammon than all the able-bodied beggars in the whole kingdom. Those who are able-bodied and rich, we tolerate. But those who are able-bodied and beg, we can under no circumstances endure. Among Christians, however, the misery and want of the poor should not be of lesser importance than the might and power of the rich. If we are lenient on one group, we should at least excuse the other as well.[21]

Consideration 7

Although there are some unoccupied and deviant men who have fallen into poverty because of their laziness and inactivity, and perhaps others who pretend to be poor, we must add that there are nevertheless very many who have genuinely been made poor by the rich. For as we read in Ecclesiasticus, "A wild ass is the prey of the lion in the wilderness: so are the poor the pastures and food of the rich."[22] Consequently, it would not be inappropriate to compensate the injuries done to the truly poor by tolerating the pretenders. I do not know whether my compassion for the poor has made me go further in my opposition to the rich than I had set out. But I believe that I have said nothing

---

[21] Ed. note: The Latin text, "*ut saltem inter illos, his etiam parceremus,*" is cryptic and differs from the Spanish version: "*para que a bueltas de los males de los unos, se dissimulassen los de los otros.*" Soto, *Relecciones y opúsculos*, II-2, 291.

[22] Ecclesiasticus 13:23 (or 13:19).

which is not either written in God's Holy Word or commonly said by everyone.

Neither can I silently pass over the fact that whenever some public office or (which is worse) ecclesiastical benefice is bestowed on someone, the dignity of that person or his merits are not at all taken into account, even though Christ, the founder of benefices, wanted us to consider that of the utmost importance. And yet for a beggar to be allowed to ask for bread, a large investigation and official approval are required.

Last of all I fear that by means of our current level of diligence and method of examining and expelling the able-bodied poor, we will not completely reach our intended goal, which is, in my view, to have no robbers and wicked men in the republic. For those who leave a city do not return directly to their native land but wander through towns and regions. Consequently, those who were once stealing mildly and in small quantities by feigning mendicity start to train themselves in more audacious thefts and robberies. We cannot punish them all by hanging. In case of other kinds of vices, lesser evils are permitted in order to avoid greater evils. Augustine said that "if you take away prostitutes, all things will be contaminated by fornication."[23] Some bandits might come from among the able-bodied beggars, and we should take action against them following a certain rationale and method. Nevertheless, following Augustine's saying, it is also appropriate and conducive to the public good to temper some of the severity exercised in this matter. That will allow us to avoid able-bodied beggars becoming the ablest of robbers.

---

[23] Ed. note: Augustine, *De ordine* II.4, 12 (PL 32:1000): "*Aufer meretrices de rebus humanis, turbaveris omnia libidinibus.*"

10

The Evaluation of the Life of the Poor

The second thing which is inspected in the poor before they are allowed to beg concerns their life and conduct, whether they keep concubines or have been infected by some other moral contagion, or whether they confess at regular intervals and observe other things of this kind which are required of all Christian men. Of course, there can be no one who disapproves of zealousness in taking care of such matters. For there is no class among the mortals to which we do not owe fraternal correction.[1] But as often as the holy fathers may have written on almsgiving, they never wanted the acts of mercy that are owed to the poor to be made conditional upon such strong obligations of justice.

Mercy

As a matter of fact, the word "alms," or *eleemosyna* (which is in fact a Greek word[2]) means the same as *misericordia*, that is "mercy." Corporal

---

[1] Ed. note: In short, "fraternal correction" denotes the duty of every Christian to talk to his brother about his misbehavior. See Wim Decock, *Theologians and Contract Law: The Moral Transformation of the Ius Commune (ca. 1500–1650)* (Leiden: Brill, 2013), 88–92.

[2] Ed. note: The Latin *eleemosyna* (used frequently by Soto) is a transliteration of the Greek ἐλεημοσύνη. The Greek word ἔλεος means "mercy, pity, compassion."

works of mercy have the misery and poverty of the poor as their material object. The office of that mercy is to again and again feed the hungry, clothe the naked, and shelter the foreigner.[3] According to the saints, it was unnecessary to conduct an investigation into a poor person before exhibiting mercy toward him. They only verified that he was a needy beggar. Spiritual works of mercy have a separate foundation, namely, fraternal correction. As for works of justice involving the repression of wrongdoers, they specifically belong to the ministers of justice.[4] For it is one thing to be merciful and another to punish wrongdoers.

I ask you, Most Christian Prince, to listen to the opinion of Chrysostom on this matter, which he expressed many times in other places but especially in his second sermon on Lazarus the beggar.[5] Already in his time, the rich hoped to conceal their own greed by expelling the poor and claiming to exercise the duty of fraternal correction. To show his disapproval, Chrysostom added the following words in a speech that becomes stronger as it develops:

> The wise Abraham did not examine what kind of people passersby were, nor where they came from, like we do now, but received all passersby without discrimination. For he who shows kindness should not demand an account of their life, but should relieve their poverty and satisfy their needs. A poor man has but a single defense: that he lives in want, and finds himself in a situation of need. May you demand nothing more from him. Even if he were the most wicked of all, if he is in need of necessary provisions, we should satisfy his hunger. Thus did Christ also command us, when he said: "Be similar to your Father, who is in heaven, who causes his sun to rise on the good and the evil, and sends down rain on the just and

---

[3] Ed. note: Three of the seven corporal works of mercy. Cf. Isa. 58:7; Matt. 25:35–38.

[4] As we have noted shortly before. Ed. note: See ch. 9, cons. 1, pp. 67–68.

[5] Chrysostom, *De Lazaro concio secunda* (PG 48:981–92).

the unjust."[6] The merciful man is a harbor for those who are in need. For all who experience a shipwreck are received and rescued by the harbor, whether they are good or evil. In short, whoever they may be, as long as they are in danger, the harbor receives them in its places of refuge. You, therefore, if you see a man who has experienced the shipwreck of poverty, do not judge him, do not examine how he has lived his life, but relieve his distress. Why give yourself extra work by examining the poor? God has freed you from the anxieties and curiosity involved in such an undertaking. How many things would so many people have to explain, and how annoyed would they be, if God had commanded that we should first inquire meticulously into the life and deeds of each individual, and only then give alms? But in reality, he has freed us from all that curiosity. So why do we invite unnecessary trouble? It is one thing to be a judge; it is a different thing to give alms. We call it "alms" because we give it to the undeserving as well. That is also why Paul said, "Do what is good to all men, but especially to those who belong to the household of the faith."[7] If we inquire and investigate the unworthy, not even the worthy will easily come to us. Conversely, if we provide support to the unworthy, undoubtedly the worthy (including those whose virtue compensates the malice of all the unworthy) shall also come into our hands. This is what occurred to the blessed Abraham, who was not in the least curious about the kind of people who were passing by. What happened in the end is that he received angels on account of his hospitality.[8] Consequently, we should imitate him, and together with him his descendant Job, for the latter imitated the magnanimity of his ancestor most diligently. That is why he said, "My door was always open to anyone that came."[9] That it was open to one person did not mean that it was closed to another: rather, it was open

---

[6] Ed. note: Matt. 5:45.

[7] Gal. 6:10.

[8] Ed. note: Gen. 18:1–8.

[9] Job 31:32.

to everyone without discrimination. We too should imitate that example by investigating no more than is required. For a poor person only has to be needy in order to be worthy of receiving alms. If someone would approach us with the recommendation of his poverty, let us not curiously scrutinize him further. We should not give someone something on account of his behavior, but on account of him being a human being. For we should not have pity on someone on account of his virtue, but on account of his misfortune. Undoubtedly, doing this will allow us to acquire abundant mercy from the Lord for ourselves, and to become, as individuals, highly deserving of the favor he bestows on us. For if we begin to verify the worthiness and conduct of those who are our fellow servants, God will do the same to us. And while we eagerly demand our fellow servants to account for their way of life, we ourselves will lose the favor of God in heaven. For he said, "For in the same way you have judged, so will you be judged."[10]

Perhaps Saint Chrysostom has come under the suspicion of conceding far too much to the poor, since that pious man was inflamed with mercy. His writings dress the poor in precious attire, making their class shine with titles of honor. So let us see whether Ambrose agrees with Chrysostom. In his book *On Naboth*, he discusses how alms should be given and says the following: "Do not verify what each and every poor person deserves to receive. Mercy is not accustomed to passing judgment on merits, but to relieving needs—to helping the poor, not to examining their rightfulness. For it is written[11]: 'Blessed is he who has regard for the needy and the poor.'"[12] Here no distinction is made between poor people who are good and those who are bad.

I believe someone might want to hear a testimony from Saint Augustine, whose genius lies in disputing and analyzing subjects very concisely. Let me therefore add the testimony of Augustine in his

---

[10] Chrysostom, *De Lazaro concio secunda* 5–6 (PG 48:989–90).

[11] Ed. note: Ps. 40:2.

[12] Ambrose, *De Nabuthe Jezraelita*, 8, 40 (PL 14:743).

exposition on Psalm 102 regarding the verse "the Lord performs acts of mercy."[13] There he teaches that God performs no act of mercy except to those who are themselves merciful, according to the word of the Lord, "Blessed are the merciful: for they themselves shall obtain mercy."[14] He also adds how far our mercy should go, lest we extend it only to a friend and not to an enemy.[15] For it is said, "Love your enemies. Do good to those that hate you."[16] And Proverbs reads, "If your enemy should be hungry, give him something to eat."[17] But enemies, especially if they are enemies of the good, cannot be good. Therefore if there is mercy for enemies, it is not mercy's duty to make a distinction between good and evil. For the merciful God causes his sun to rise over the good and the evil.[18] And so Christ, the Father of Mercy, put no limit on mercy but said, "Give to anyone who asks you."[19]

Augustine, however, presents some evidence from Ecclesiasticus, which on the face of it seems to contradict that opinion. For we read, "If you do good works, know to whom you do them. Do good to the just, and you shall be repaid, for the Highest hates sinners, and has mercy upon the penitent. You, therefore, give to the merciful and support no sinner. Give to the good and receive no sinner. Do good to the humble, and do not give to the ungodly."[20] See how many words that sage in Ecclesiasticus repeats and accumulates to convince us to be benefactors to no one besides the just. But then Augustine goes on to qualify this statement, since nothing must contradict the gospel. Augustine says that you can accomplish both commands, namely,

---

[13] Ps. 102:6.

[14] Ed. note: Matt. 5:7.

[15] Augustine, *Enarrationes in Psalmos*, Ps. 102 (PL 36:1325–29).

[16] Ed. note: Matt. 5:44; Luke 6:27.

[17] Prov. 25:21.

[18] Ed. note: Matt. 5:45.

[19] Luke 6:30.

[20] Ecclesiasticus 12:1–6. Ed. note: The cited version is shorter than the original.

"support no sinner[21] and "give to anyone who asks you."[22] According to Augustine, if at any time a sinner asks you for something, you should not give him something because he is a sinner but because he is in need. If you intend to alleviate the need and misery of a poor person, you do not intend to foster sin. So much for Augustine's opinion.[23] Therefore, the sage in Ecclesiasticus tried to warn us that a poor man can be lured into sin by the sheer mass of alms he receives. He then becomes a reprobate, and the benefits conferred to him become the seeds and fomenters of his vices. In that case, those goods should be taken away from him for the sake of fraternal correction.

Augustine wrote about this in a letter to Vincentius the Donatist, which has been included in *Non omnis*, a canon in the *Decretum*. It says, "Taking away the bread from a hungry man who disregards justice when he does not have to worry about food benefits that man more than breaking bread for him and thereby making him acquiesce in his detachment from justice."[24] This canon should be understood as applying in cases where it has been established with full certainty that the alms are more of a danger than a benefit to the poor person. We are not allowed to scrutinize the poor in any other way. Rather, we should observe another lesson of Augustine which appears in his book *On the Five Heresies*. After commending the hospitality of Abraham and Lot, who showed hospitality toward all people without discrimination and were rewarded by receiving angels as guests, he adds, "Christians, learn to receive guests without discrimination: otherwise the one whom you have closed your door on and whom you have refused to treat with humanity might be God himself."[25] This principle should also be upheld in the practice of other works of piety.

---

[21] Ecclesiasticus 12:4.

[22] Luke 6:30.

[23] Augustine, *Enarrationes in Psalmos*, Ps. 102 (PL 36:1325–29, esp. 1327).

[24] Dec. Grat. C.5 q.5 c.2.

[25] Ps.-Augustine, *De quinque haeresibus* 4.5 (PL 42:1104).

Epilogue

Therefore what can be gathered from so many and such clear testimonies of the saints is, to summarize everything, that making a distinction between good and evil persons is not a duty of mercy. It is reserved to the office and ministers of justice. The essence of mercy is to relieve the plight of all men without discrimination and to come to their aid.

Now those who critically watch the conduct of the poor acted like pious and wise Christians when they wrote a preamble at the head of their articles. For in it they praised the immeasurable love, kindness, and clemency of Christ our Savior toward us and reminded us most piously that we should repay him through his poor for those extraordinary services of charity which he performed for all of us. In light of the summary of the preceding discussion, it has to be considered whether the laws which they wrote under that preface are sufficiently suitable and in agreement with it. For these laws state first that those who are vagabonds and pseudo-paupers should be banished from the city. Second, that nothing should be granted to beggars who are foreign except their passage. And third, that the life and conduct of native beggars should be assessed diligently. All of this is to be skillfully carried out by officials and praetors. We should furthermore consider whether that pious preamble could not be followed by something finer and more appropriate, ensuring that we truly are (as often as we have given Christ our names and our word) merciful and kind toward all men in general, without discrimination.

For that is what Abraham did, whom Christ deemed worthy to call his father. In the same way did Christ's almsgiver Tobias[26] give instructions to his son, saying, "Do not turn your face away from a poor person, so that the Lord will not turn his face away from you."[27] Christ's servant Job boasted that he never denied a poor person what he wanted.[28] His saints compare mercy to a harbor which receives

---

[26] Ed. note: Called Tobit in most contemporary Bible translations.

[27] Tob. 4:7.

[28] Job 31:16.

and rescues all who are shipwrecked without discrimination.[29] The same thing was preached by the Master when he said, "Give to anyone who asks you."[30] Following that reasoning, when Christ fed the great multitude in the wasteland, he excluded no vagabonds and did not treat the good and the wicked differently.[31]

Mercy

The word "mercy" means "to bestow a benefit to the unworthy," since granting something to the worthy is a matter of justice. That is why God is merciful for causing his sun to rise on the good and the evil, and sending down rain on the just and the unjust.[32] Herein, Christ wanted our righteousness to surpass the righteousness of the Pharisees so that we would love not only our friends, as they did, but our enemies as well. Finally, the apostle commends Christ's indescribable mercy toward us in the words, "When we were still sinners, Christ died for us."[33]

It is true that those who devise these constitutions for the poor could have a pious intention. They might be just men, as long as they are not so excessively just that they usurp for themselves the praetors' duty to act against wrongdoers. However, they have very little reason to believe that the mercy which they demonstrate is pure and flawless, since true mercy does not distinguish between the worthy and unworthy. All other things being equal, it follows from the order of charity that in giving alms, we should give preference to good persons over the bad, and to the better over the worse. However, to scrutinize merits meticulously does not befit a merciful man. Neither can it be merciful to not only give nothing to sinners, but to also prohibit them from asking others who might perhaps grant them what you refuse. They have undoubtedly learned the words of Christ in the Gospel of Matthew: "Whenever you enter a house, say, 'Peace be to this house.'

---

[29] Ed. note: Chrysostom, *De Lazaro concio secunda* 5–6 (PG 48:989).

[30] Luke 6:30.

[31] John 6:2–11.

[32] Matt. 5:45.

[33] Rom. 5:8–9.

And should that house be worthy, your peace will come upon it; but should it not be worthy, your peace will return to you."[34] By the same token when it comes to almsgiving, a poor person might not deserve to receive alms, but his benefactor still awaits a reward with God.

Regarding the question of the equity and justice of the fourth article, especially the harshness of forcing the poor to confess their sins, I would prefer to admit my ignorance than to consent entirely to such a harsh sanction. It is obvious that we have to instruct the poor about the necessity of this sacrament and to encourage them to take it, but it is not a sign of piety to leave them in such dire straits by prohibiting them from begging unless they have confessed.

First, besides the fact that it would constitute an intolerable law, to impose the sacrament of confession under pain of capital punishment would certainly also incite hatred toward this most holy sacrament. Indeed, to forbid beggars to beg constitutes capital punishment, seeing that they have no other livelihood. Therefore, it is not allowed to force them to go to confession under pain of that punishment. They should merely be persuaded into receiving the sacrament of confession. I would like to ask the rich whether they would not bear the following situation with much difficulty. Imagine that confession was declared compulsory for the rich by a law prohibiting them from ever eating bread after Easter unless they have made a prior confession. Would they die of hunger rather than cry out in protest? I do not think so. What gives you the right, then, you rich people, to be so harsh in your attitude toward the miserable?

They respond that among the miserable there are people who have not been to confession for a whole decade. But likewise there are also many people of that sort among the rich, but they are not pushed so harshly toward confession. "Yet the rich are not asking for the goods of others, and I do not want to donate my goods to poor people who have not gone to confession." Here the main point of this issue is being covered up: it is the rut in which those people always get stuck. Here I would like to request their attention. For even though I want to avoid arguing about the extent to which the needy possess a direct

---

34 Matt. 10:11–13.

Deliberation on the Cause of the Poor

right to your goods—there are holy fathers who believed this, but we hesitate to include it in our discourse—the following is crystal clear and cannot be denied by anyone.

Every poor man in a situation of necessity, even less than grave necessity, has a right to ask for alms, and that right is the same as everyone's right to possess his own goods. The right of the poor man is perhaps even stronger since he is in a situation of greater necessity. I am not speaking of a right to take goods against the will of the owner (unless the pauper is in a situation of extreme necessity), but of a right to ask, to request, and to implore. Therefore there is no one, of whatever authority he might be, who can deprive the poor of this right, except on account of a crime for which he could also have confiscated the goods of the rich; and I would even dare to say on account of a crime for which he could have condemned the rich to die of hunger.

For he who deprives the poor of their right to ask for alms pushes them toward starvation. Therefore, imagine some exceedingly legalistic person who decides to give no food to the poor unless they have first been approved and gone to confession—as if that food were the most holy sacrament of the Eucharist. Then he should not also deprive the miserable man of his right and capacity to travel around, for perhaps that man might find someone better instructed in the laws of mercy who would be willing to offer him bread.

Moreover, if the uneducated multitude of the poor is so harshly coerced to go to confession, would you not agree, Most Noble Prince, that something would happen which we have to avoid at all costs? For in their attempts to avoid choking from hunger, many people might start to confess false and fictitious things and thereby contaminate the sacrament.

The holy fathers of the synod[35] only ordered us to partake once a year of the sacrament of confession, which is based on divine law, even though they understood perfectly well that they could have enforced

---

[35] Ed. note: This was decided in canon 21 (*Omnis utriusque sexus fidelis*) of the Fourth Lateran Council (1215), convened by Pope Innocent III. See Giuseppe Alberigo and Alberto Melloni, eds., *The General Councils of Latin Christendom: From Constantinople IV to Pavia-Siena (869–1424)*, Corpus

the precept with greater punishments. This would perhaps have led to fewer people transgressing it by never going to confession. Nonetheless, they worried that the fear of the gravest punishment would lead some to commit sacrilege against the sacrament by confessing falsehoods. They therefore considered it sufficient to refuse entry into the church and access to a church burial to those who never confess.[36]

Although Christians would consider this a harsher punishment than extreme hunger, nevertheless it does not frighten men as much as temporal punishment and is not terrifying enough to cause them to make a fake confession. Furthermore, since one of the sixteen qualities and conditions which ought to accompany the sacrament of confession is that it should be voluntary, I fail to understand how so rigorously forcing men to confess could be reconciled with this requirement.

The Correction of the Poor

As far as the correction of the poor is concerned, the following rules have been laid down in the articles in a most pious way—provided that they are enforced with due diligence. First, the poor's little ones should be taken away from the care of their parents and be assigned to guardians or entrusted to artisans and craftsmen. Next, the poor should be forced to hear public sermons from time to time in which they might be taught religion and virtue and receive admonishment and exhortation. It would be best for their well-being to appoint some men of good conduct under whose care and charge they should be placed. Clearly, we would then combine spiritual with corporal works of mercy and follow the example of God who carefully sustains the corporal life while also organizing the spiritual life with his laws, counsels, examples, and admonishments, leading men to what is good and virtuous.

Christianorum. Conciliorum Oecumenicorum Generaliumque Decreta. Editio Critica, II/1 (Turnhout: Brepols, 2013), 178.

[36] Ed. note: Dec. Greg. 5.38.12.

Hidden Sins Should Not Be Uncovered

First of all, I consider it necessary to warn about the method used in investigating and exploring the conduct of the poor, especially of those who do not want to disclose their mendicancy publicly. As I see it, far from handing alms to them for free, alms are sold to them for the highest price. After all, men would rather suffer from extreme hunger than to have their mendicancy publicly revealed, which is certainly true of the Spanish, who consider honor more valuable than life. Nevertheless, when the poor are registered, their privacy[37] is not taken into account. The nobles who have been entrusted with this task investigate the poor publicly, accompanied by a large following of servants. Many paupers would prefer to receive no alms instead of having to purchase them for such a high price. If the famous rule of almsgiving that "our left hand should not know what our right hand is doing"[38] is to be observed in any nation, it should first of all be observed in Spain. For that is what Ambrose, Nicholas, Chrysostom, and the other holy fathers practiced very conscientiously.

But what is far worse, not to say more unjust: they sometimes inquire into the hidden sins[39] of the poor before bestowing even the most miserable alms to them, without respect for due process.[40]

In one of our lectures, published under the title *On the Method of Concealing and Revealing a Secret*, we argued to the best of our ability that no one has the right to inquire into sins and to scrutinize them, unless strong indications point to them or some rumor raises an outcry.[41] But even when those preconditions are manifestly met,

---

[37] *ratio secreti.*

[38] Ed. note: Matt. 6:3.

[39] *crimina.* Ed. note: The Spanish version reads *peccados.* In the remainder of the discussion, the Latin words *crimina* and *peccata* are used interchangeably.

[40] *praeter iuris ordinem.*

[41] Soto, *Relectio de ratione tegendi et detegendi secretum*, membrum 2, q. 6, concl. 1. Ed. note: Domingo de Soto, *Relecciones y opúsculos*, II-1, *El abuso de los juramentos. La ocultación y revelación de secretos*, ed. A. O. Fernández-Largo (Salamanca: San Esteban, 2000), 368.

the sins of the rich are still not always subject to any investigation. Much greater care and diligence is invested, by contrast, in revealing the secret sins of the poor than in alleviating their miseries. Their condition must be pitied since they have to bear such a large risk for their reputation in order to eventually receive only a couple of pennies. Awareness is needed about the fact that those wretched men, stricken by hardship and miseries, commit sins very easily just to console their mind, while the rich commit far greater sins because of their luxury and abundance of fortune. If being aware of this is not reason enough to show mercy to those poor, miserable sinners, what worldly punishments could we possibly demand for them that are harsher than what they are already suffering on account of their calamities, adversities, and afflictions? Excluded from honors, devoid of joy, naked, without bed, without roof, sustaining a continuous war with cold, heat, and, in the end, hunger, which is the most atrocious punishment of all. For the prophet says that "those who are killed by the sword have it better than those who die of hunger."[42] When they have been finally deprived of all things that render men happy in this life and are practically expelled from the world, they lead a life in no way more desirable than death.

Moreover—and this is among men most inhumane—so many of the needy are pushed by poverty and mendicancy into crime. The greedy rich act cruelly toward the poor in two ways: first, it is their greed and tenacity which cause them to commit sins, and second, they in turn take occasion from these offenses to feed their greed, relentless as they are. Since the goal is to correct the ruinous habits of the poor and to bring them to their senses, more beneficial foresight would be exercised and better provisions made if we would soften their minds, entice them, and get them back on the right track by conferring temporal benefits and support. By taking away their food, the only thing we achieve is that the vices of those who are desperate and have lost all hope are set loose.

I do not want to say this to favor those who have gone astray, but in the first place to avoid that we are so eager to apply the principles of

---

[42] Lam. 4:9.

justice to the poor that we do that before helping them and granting them mercy, and end up being unjust in the process. I also want to avoid that the application of so much care and skill in suppressing vagabonds, repelling foreigners, and inquiring into the citizens' lives and conduct eventually leads to a diminishment of the resources attributed to almsgiving. I could never grow tired of restating again and again that if alms become rarer and smaller because of the investigations of the rich, the latter would actually have been better off had they never come up with the idea in the first place. For even if the total amount of alms increased, they would still fall short of reaching a level which is just.

In fact, Christians are required to give alms at innumerable occasions. For instance if you want to curtail the invasive fire of vices, the wise man says, "In the same way as water extinguishing a flaming fire, so do alms resist sins."[43] And if you desire to redeem the sins you have already committed, listen to the prophet Daniel: "Redeem your sins with alms, and your iniquities with works of charity for the poor."[44] But if you want to completely wash away even the smallest vestiges of sin, heed the following commandment of Christ: "Give alms, and see, all things are clean unto you."[45] If your soul has been cleansed, it still has to prepare its traversal through this life with ample food and provisions. That is why the wise man in Ecclesiasticus says, "The alms of a man are like a purse with him, which will preserve the grace of that man like the apple of the eye."[46] If you have to preserve your treasures from moth, rust, and robbers, entrust them to the poor. For Christ spoke about alms when he said, "Do not hoard treasures for yourself on earth, where rust and moth destroy, and where thieves

---

[43] Ed. note: Ecclesiasticus 3:33.

[44] Ed. note: Dan. 4:24. On the seminal role of this passage in the Judeo-Christian construction of the metaphor of sin as a debt that must be repaid (and which can be cancelled through almsgiving), see G. A. Anderson, *Charity: The Place of the Poor in the Biblical Tradition* (New Haven: Yale University Press, 2013), 1–12.

[45] Ed. note: Luke 11:41.

[46] Ecclesiasticus 17:18.

break in and steal. But hoard treasures for yourself in heaven, where neither moth nor rust destroy, and where thieves do not break in and steal."[47] But to the rich of this world he says, using a hyperbole, that it is just as impossible for them to enter the kingdom of heaven as it is for a camel to pass through the eye of a needle.[48] The only remedy he left to the rich was to make friends among the poor by spending the mammon of their iniquity, so that these friends may give them access to heaven.[49] That is why Paul instructed Timothy to tell the rich of this world to be generous,[50] for "those who want to become rich fall into temptation and into the snare of the devil."[51] What is more, if you not only wish to be received into the eternal dwellings but also yearn for that eternal glory of companionship with the princes and most perfect in the kingdom of heaven (as we all should), Christ showed you no other way: you should sell all that you have, distribute the proceeds among the poor, and follow him.[52] And with that, more than enough should have been said about the inquiries, verifications, and investigations which are described in the first, third, and fourth articles. For we have explained the second and the fifth articles in the first part of this deliberation.[53]

---

[47] Matt. 6:19–20.

[48] Matt. 19:24.

[49] Luke 16:9.

[50] 1 Tim. 6:18.

[51] 1 Tim. 6:9.

[52] Ed. note: Matt. 19:21.

[53] The second article concerns foreign beggars and is discussed in chs. 4 and 5. The fifth article about the pilgrims to Santiago is discussed in ch. 6.

11

ON THE MANNER OF ASKING FROM DOOR TO DOOR

In accordance with our plan, we have reached the right moment for a thorough investigation into the article which has received the most attention among all the articles that have circulated. It is about whether it would be just and fair, and to use the words of Paul, "expedient and edifying,"[1] to keep the poor away from the front doors of Christians and to feed them in hospices instead of allowing them to publicly display their own hardships and calamities before the eyes of Christians. I may be wrong, but this issue is subject to more controversy than the authors of the articles assume.

First, we have to discern four kinds of beggars. There are some who beg because of an everlasting vow, such as the members of religious orders. Their mendicancy consists of having nothing of their own and of living on alms from day to day.[2] There is no question of their legitimacy here, for the heresies of those who railed against the mendicant orders were condemned long ago.

Others can be beggars not because of a solemn vow, but because they have given away their own possessions to the poor for the sake of maintaining the extraordinary virtue of humility and have lowered themselves to that most humble condition of mendicancy. That is what

---

[1] Ed. note: 1 Cor. 6:12; 10:23.

[2] *In diem vivere*. Ed. note: e.g., Cicero, *De oratore* II.40, 169.

is written of Saint Alexius, a Roman patrician, as well as Arsenius in *Lives of the Fathers*.[3] Jerome also commemorated Fabiola in his letter to Oceanus because she first showered the poor with her riches and then wanted to live on the alms of poor people.[4] Saint Thomas therefore commends the same kind of humility in his *Summa*.[5] Consequently, although this practice has not been so common in this age, there is no reason to condemn it. Rather, if their mode of life has been approved, they must be permitted to go from door to door.

The third kind of beggars are the pilgrims, and the fourth kind are those forced to ask for alms out of poverty and want. It is mainly with regard to these last two kinds that there now exists quarrel and controversy.

The First Conclusion

To make a distinction between the rigor of justice on the one hand and equity and mercy on the other, the first conclusion of this article should be the following. The prince, in whose hand lies the power over the republic, has the right and the authority to prohibit beggars from going from door to door and asking for alms on condition that he makes sure that there are other ways to provide them with adequate food, clothing, and other necessities in accordance with their rank. Unless that condition has been met, he is unable to forbid begging in any way. Neither can anyone object to this conclusion with arguments that meet the standards of probability. After all, this is too evident to require many textual witnesses. For as Aristotle states in his *Ethics*,[6] since the prince is by natural and divine law put in charge of the republic in order to render citizens good, he can command anything by edict as long as it is a work of virtue. He can also immediately suppress acts which are vices and sins. Now as long as they are in need,

---

[3] Ed. note: For Arsenius, see *Vita Patrum sive Historiae Eremiticae* V, libel. 6 (PL 73:888).

[4] Jerome, *Epistula 77 ad Oceanum*, 9 (PL 22:696).

[5] Thomas Aquinas, *Summa theologiae* II-2, q. 187, a. 5, resp.

[6] Aristotle, *Nicomachean Ethics* II.1 (1103b).

the needy do not commit a sin by going from door to door to ask for alms. But as soon as their necessities have been provided for, they do sin by begging for other people's property under the pretext of their poverty. Therefore when a prince or a republic has provided for their basic necessities, he can inhibit the poor from begging door to door. Otherwise, this is in no way possible.

I certainly believe that the prince has the legal authority to do this. However, going beyond what is just, a republic which provides the poor with abundant supplies and ensures that they no longer have to wander through the city by going from door to door makes the evangelical truth and the charity of Christ—who is our head and of whom we are the members—shine much more brightly within its confines. For how could that law which orders us to love our neighbors as ourselves be practiced in a community in which there are some who have an abundance and excess of all sorts of goods and others who are extremely needy and reduced to mendicancy? There is a famous adage by a natural philosopher who responded to a very rich man proclaiming to be on the friendliest of terms with a very poor person. He supposedly told him that it is not credible for any friendship to exist between a very rich man and a beggar. The divine apostle, whom I mentioned shortly before,[7] expressed the same view in the following words: "if someone possesses worldly wealth," etc.[8] Indeed, long before he proclaimed it in the gospel, God already inscribed this natural law of friendship onto the hearts of all mortals.

The pagans definitely expressed it in that common proverb: "Friends have all things in common, and a friend is an alter ego."[9] Some believe that Pythagoras is the author of that expression. Socrates inferred the following from it: since good men are the friends of the gods, and all

---

[7] Ed. note: ch. 8, pp. 60–61.

[8] 1 John 3:17.

[9] Ed. note: For examples of the common proverb that "friends share everything in common," see Aristotle, *Nicomachean Ethics* VIII.9 (1159b); Diogenes Laertius, *The Lives of Eminent Philosophers* VIII.10; and Cicero, *De officiis* I.16, 51. Note that the 1547 Latin text contains a typographical error, *alter ergo* instead of *alter ego*.

things belong to the gods, good men also have a right to all things. The apostles adhered to this law as well, and they were interpreters of the divine and promulgators of the law of the gospel, which constitutes the perfection of all natural law. They preached this law at least in Jerusalem and the surrounding province of Judea when they began their baptisms. As is written in the Acts,[10] all those who received a new, Christian name through baptism were persuaded to sell their goods and to put the money at the feet of the apostles. The apostles then redistributed the wealth among individual Christians, to each according to his need. That is why, as the story goes, "there was not one needy person among them."[11] During the time when this holy and common practice was still observed, however short it was, a new Christian named Ananias hid, with the knowledge of his wife, the money for which he had sold their possessions. Peter rebuked him so harshly for his greed that he collapsed with fear and died.[12] The model proposed in the Acts served as an example for the later monasteries of the religious orders whose members live a life in common and restore that charity of the followers of Christ. As is told in the Acts of the Apostles, seven men of good conduct were appointed to serve the tables of the widows, orphans, and other poor people, and Stephen was the first among them.[13] I am saying this to prove the following proposition: the creation of a stable legal framework[14] guaranteeing the poor all basic necessities would be, if possible, merely a matter of Christian charity.

The Second Conclusion

I nevertheless add a second conclusion to the previous one. Considering the way things are now, it is not possible to take such good care of the poor that they could be lawfully prohibited from door-to-door

---

[10] Ed. note: Acts 4:32–35.

[11] Ed. note: Acts 4:34.

[12] Ed. note: Acts 5:1–5.

[13] Ed. note: Acts 6:1–6.

[14] *certa lege.*

begging. What I would call "possible" is that which the theologians call "morally possible," and which Aristotle in his work *On the Heavens*[15] considered to be "something which could very well happen." To corroborate this conclusion, about two or three principles need to be explained.

The first principle states that no method or limit in giving alms has been prescribed by precept or law in the gospel.[16] Which is to say, what percentage of their goods men have to give away in alms has not been predetermined to be, for instance, a tenth or a twentieth. Neither has the number of poor people which certain men or a certain republic have to support ever been defined, nor is it prescribed which needs we need to meet. We are only reminded of the fact that we will always have the poor with us.[17] Christ our Savior has enticed us very strongly with his promises and has terrified us with his threats that we might love our neighbors as ourselves and within our means allow no one to be in need.

The second principle, which we mentioned above,[18] is the following. Men cannot be obliged by human law to give alms beyond what is prescribed by the gospel, except for hospice endowments and perhaps other sources of income allocated specifically to the poor, which we have to treat like the property of the poor. Rather, as is currently the custom, anyone is free to give as many alms as he wants. Besides, even among the community of Christians there are extremely stingy men whom no beggar can persuade to give alms, not even with the greatest persistence. In fact, very rare are those who behave in accordance with the truth of the gospel and give alms in proportion to their own ability and the need of the miserable.

I add a third principle which should be taken into consideration especially by those who are planning to confine so many poor beggars.

---

[15] *Arist. primo de coelo.* Ed. note: Aristotle, *De caelo* I.11 (281a).

[16] Ed. note: "In the gospel" is not found in the Venetian edition, but we do find it in the original Spanish text. Soto, *Relecciones y opúsculos*, II-2, 321: "*en el Evangelio.*"

[17] Ed. note: Matt. 26:11; Mark 14:7; John 12:8.

[18] Ed. note: ch. 4, arg. 2, pp. 30–32.

Anyone depriving beggars of the right to ask for alms or anyone responsible for that deprivation becomes indebted to them. He will have to lessen their miseries and to relieve their needs. We are talking of those needs which the poor would likely have been able to meet by begging (it would have been "morally probable," as they say). For example, let us assume that there are a hundred or a thousand legitimate poor people in a city, and that it is not possible to look sufficiently after their needs with less than two hundred gold ducats. Let us further assume that those poor are in all likelihood able to collect that amount if they are allowed to beg from door to door. I believe that the aforementioned principle then implies the following: for individuals, there is no obligation as a matter of justice to give to those who have the permission to beg, but to do so is an act of mercy. For a republic, however, or at least for the ruler who prohibited them from begging, an obligation does exist as a matter of justice to cater to the needs of those whom he does not allow to beg and to spend the entire sum of two hundred ducats to their advantage. This is obvious, for the poor have the right to beg, and whoever deprives them of their proper right is obliged to compensate their loss according to the maxim from Roman law that "he who created the cause of the damage is deemed to have created the damage."[19]

On the basis of these principles, we can now prove the second conclusion. According to the third principle, we have to provide beggars with basic necessities before we can lawfully prohibit them from asking for alms. For we owe beggars those necessities according to justice. To provide for so many necessities, however, is not "morally possible," as they call it. It is therefore not right to prohibit them from begging. Certainly, the first and second principles have sufficiently demonstrated that it is not possible to provide the confined poor with enough to meet the requirements of justice. On the one hand, there is no way to determine the exact number of poor people or to quantify their needs, since both natives and foreigners have the right to beg,

---

[19] Ed. note: This maxim is derived from Dig. 9.2.30.3.

as we have said earlier.[20] On the other hand, citizens cannot be forced to give alms. How then, I ask, could the republic pay back the debt which it incurred by prohibiting begging? The matter is all the more urgent since the necessities of the poor include not only food but also clothing, a bed, and even extra household items and additional food in case the pauper has a family. If the poor are allowed to beg, no one is obliged to impart alms to them unless in cases of extreme or perhaps grave necessity. But since they are prohibited from begging, that which was an act of mercy becomes an obligation of justice. For he who deprives the poor of their right, as I said shortly ago, incurs a debt which amounts to all that a poor person might have acquired and collected by begging.

The second reason is that I am unable to understand what reasoning and measurement should be applied to distribute the rations and portions effectively among the confined poor. For among the poor there can be a single person for whom the portions of three others are not even sufficient because of his specific physical constitution and state of health. If food rations of equal size are distributed to everyone, that person will inevitably have to fight continuously with hunger. Yet before, he had the right to ask for alms until satisfaction. After all, who would not satisfy even a slave's hunger with at least some bread, apart from someone who would rightly be convicted of inhumanity and cruelty?

Although the third reason has not received the first and most prominent place in this deliberation, neither is it the least: After they began to put this method of almsgiving into practice, they learned from experience that the fixed portions and rations which are distributed to the poor barely suffice to satisfy a man with bread, supposing that his stomach has not yet grown too weak. Neither do his rations allow him to buy some fruit or vegetables, or we would grant it, a little piece of meat once a week. But are the rich not content with distinguishing themselves from the poor by their ability to feed themselves with expensive poultry and indulge in what they eat, while the poor do not

---

[20] Ed. note: Chapters 4 and 5 are dedicated to the defense of "foreign beggars."

have that possibility at all? Is it really necessary to add another unjust condition for the miserable, on top of everything else, by also taking away their liberty to lift their own spirits—so afflicted by misfortunes—with the food which God and nature granted to the human race? Although a poor man, I say, consumes only a cheap and meager diet, he finds strength in the possibility and liberty of sometimes stumbling upon a house where a kind man sits at the table who gives him a small dish, fruits, wine, or a similar delicacy. Such food is often even granted to slaves. I will refrain from mentioning those banquets which are frequent, splendid, and disgusting at the same time. There the leftovers first fill up the stomachs of the slaves and are then thrown to the dogs. Why are the doors of those palaces not open to the poor?

For if we believe certain grammarians, the verb "to open" (*pando*) expresses the notion that the doors used to be opened after finishing a banquet in order to give bread (*panis*) to the needy, even among pagans to whom Christ never preached almsgiving. Another explanation of the word *pando* is that a temple of Ceres always stood open[21] so that bread could be given to the needy.

Moreover, it is of course not very safe to place judgment on the poor, in which their lives are at stake, in the hands of only a few examiners. For even though two or three upright men of the highest reputation can be given preference and assigned to this work with poor people, it happens that others feel, for some reason, hatred toward the poor or are driven by false ideas—quickly circulating in places attended by the poor—and judge that some poor person does not have any legitimate reason to beg. What is such a miserable individual supposed do? That is why it was certainly a good decision by the city of Ypres in Flanders to include in its regulations the provision that beggars can explain their distress and misfortune before the ears of any city dignitary, for this ensures that those who are condemned by only a few persons are not left without any relief at all.

But on top of that, I cannot completely grasp the following from these articles: They do allow a truly poor foreigner or pilgrim to come over, and they give him lodging for at least three days. But listen,

---

[21] Ed. note: The *porta pandana*.

Greatest Prince, how much trouble they cause him before he receives a piece of bread. Suppose someone infirm, lame, or exhausted by his journey enters the city. He then has to ask where in the world he can find the official responsible for the poor. He wanders from street to street looking for his house. But when he finds it, the official is perhaps not at home, or he is asleep, and the poor man has to wait. Then when the man is given admission, he needs to answer where he comes from and where he is going. Finally, he receives nothing but a piece of paper and has to return to the quaestor or treasurer in whose offices the money is stored. Only after an entire day has been wasted is the miserable man allowed to appease his hunger and find rest. I hear that this way of proceeding is the rule in several cities, and I do not know whether foreign beggars are better taken care of elsewhere. In any event, a *xenodochium* or guesthouse where strangers are welcomed should be erected. Furthermore, there should be people at the gates of the city to guide them directly to the guesthouse.

Conclusion

I therefore believe that I must conclude what I have said in the fourth chapter:[22] that it is not possible to use such laws to provide so abundantly for the local poor that no necessity and therefore no right to leave their native land and beg elsewhere would remain. Neither does it seem possible to use such laws to help and look after the poor so adequately and sufficiently that their right to beg from door to door within their native land would cease to exist.

Perhaps I would say nothing that contradicts the law by asserting that a poor beggar is allowed to save an amount of money, however small, to improve his condition in terms of class and rank. To be sure, the miserable stand accused and are vehemently reproached for sewing gold into their clothing in order to hide it. But are there none who fill their rightful purse with other people's money? Are there none who live in luxury off that money? By contrast, the poor are deprived of all joys of life and live extremely soberly, surviving merely on bread and

---

[22] Ed. note: i.e., ch. 4, arg. 2, pp. 30–32.

vegetables in order to save some pennies that can be used in times of sickness or greater misfortune.

Moreover, anyone has the right to improve his condition and class through lawful arts and contracts. A poor man should be allowed to save a little bit of money so that he can dress and adorn himself in a more distinguished way. In this way, he might be able to serve a good and noble man, acquire the tools for exercising an art and launching a workshop, or start a small business that allows him to survive. Poor people cannot exercise that right when we confine them.

Besides, not everywhere is there an abundance of hospices to receive all the poor. And when they are locked up, the poor will fall prey to idleness and listlessness[23] even more than when they are allowed to go out and beg.

But let us pass over those kinds of reasons for the moment and return to the helm from which one ought never to remove one's hands in an affair like this. I consider it especially worthwhile to observe whether this plan increases or decreases the supply of alms. I propose that the present plan inevitably decreases and reduces the alms. Even if no other argument or testimony existed, my proposition would be manifestly proven by the fact that the authors of these institutions themselves admit it publicly. For the main reason why they commend this regulation and convince themselves that it is good is that there will be less need of almsgiving.

And truly, this is confirmed by experience. For I hear the following from other cities, and I see it with my own eyes in this city. And it has often been told to me by those who are taking care of the poor; the total amount of alms has been reduced to barely a third or fourth of what was customary before there were statutes of this sort. However, this "Achilles,"[24] whom they think fights on their side, convinces others who see the matter differently to reject this method of almsgiving. If the number of legitimate poor people was not larger, and their hardships and necessities were not greater than what the alms money raised through this method can cope with, I would admit that men,

---

[23] *accidia.*

[24] Ed. note: Metaphor for a powerful or conclusive argument.

however rich, are not obliged to give more. But in reality, there are too many poor, even if we leave out the false and pretending and only think of those who are legitimate. For their needs and misfortunes are far greater than what the donation of alms collected according to the plan can provide for. That is why the rich should be compelled to give greater alms in accordance with the law of the gospel. We should consider it rather a detriment to the rich that able-bodied beggars who have acquired alms through fraud and insolence are expelled, if what gets taken away from them is not granted in its entirety to the legitimately poor.

Besides experience, there are beyond this very clear arguments demonstrating that it is inevitable for almsgiving to become rarer through this plan.

First, there can be no bigger difference than between beggars asking for alms for their own benefit and other people asking for alms to benefit beggars. As merciful as the rich may be, they ask for alms on behalf of the poor because they seek honor. At home they have all the food they need, and they believe to have fulfilled their duty as soon as they have finished begging for alms in two or three neighborhoods. Whether they actually obtain something by asking for alms matters little to them. By contrast, when a miserable beggar begs, his nourishment itself is at stake. He is not content with just begging for alms. He actually insists to the point of becoming insolent to make sure that even the most ruthless person offers him a penny. He does not settle for begging for one hour if he needs to beg the whole day to collect enough money to survive. Do you not think, Most Merciful Prince, that this was also one of the reasons why Christ, who is most mindful of the poor, introduced that famous Gospel parable in Luke, besides the fact that he was teaching his disciples how to pray?[25] In the parable, a man went to a friend of his in the middle of the night, hoping that he would lend him three loaves of bread. But his friend's door was closed, he was lying in bed with his children, and unwilling as he was, could barely bring himself to get up in order to accommodate his friend's needs. Nevertheless, our Master says that through

---

[25] Luke 11:5–13.

his perseverance and by continuing to knock on his friend's door, he urged his friend to rise from his bed and render him the service, if not out of friendship then at least because of his stubborn insistence. If somebody would go out and ask for bread to relieve the needs of someone else, that person would certainly not insist as stubbornly to make sure that mercy is shown.

The second argument is the following. What tends to occur in bad and shameful acts, which we have to avoid, tends to occur in good acts and offices as well. For the presence of the matter and object, whether it be a virtue or a vice, possesses that immense energy to move and entice persons toward a certain action.[26] This is why it is of exceedingly great importance whether it is a rich and healthy man, with a bright face and splendid clothing, who asks you for alms, or a poor man with a pale face and dirty clothes, perhaps covered with sores, begging in the name of the mother of Christ and making humble supplications in the name of His wounds. Surely there is no one who has not found out through long experience that he very often intends to give no alms at all when he is leaving his home, but changes his mind for the better upon seeing a poor person.

Therefore, it is a principle of rhetoric that the person who suffered the injury should be presented before the eyes of the judge, if it can be done in an appropriate way, in order to rouse the judge's soul by showing his wounds. I admit that some of these poor people are frauds, but there are many more true infirmities and misfortunes than false ones. Furthermore, if a fraud deserves at any time the name of piety, it is one of those frauds which are rightly considered "pious frauds."[27] This is one good reason among others why the bishop's presence is useful and necessary to his church. For a bishop who is from hearing alone induced to send some alms to his poor will be convinced to give far more upon seeing their hardships and adversities with his own eyes.

---

[26] Ed. note: This is an oft-repeated argument in scholastic considerations about money and debt. Cf. Wim Decock, "Law, Religion, and Debt Relief: Balancing above the 'Abyss of Despair' in Early Modern Canon Law and Theology," *American Journal of Legal History* 57 (2017): 125–41.

[27] *fraus pietatis*.

Religious Mendicants

How effective it is for the person who needs something to ask for help in person can also be seen through the example of the religious mendicants who bear the likeness of that communal life of the early church, as we have said before.[28] In a convent in which they live off begging, the task of collecting all the means necessary for living according to the frugality or poverty of the religious is entrusted to just one specific person, acting justly and piously, who collects means in abundance. Of course, the reason for this abundance is that this specific person takes care of the needs of his own monastery. By contrast, if that responsibility were delegated even to ten of the most diligent and pious men, even sufficient bread to allow the monastery to survive would be difficult to acquire. That is why we religious mendicants are obliged to come to the aid of poor beggars.

The Character of the Spanish People

Furthermore, the strength of this argument is increased by the condition and character of the Spaniards. Compared to other people, the Spaniards are more easily persuaded by hearing a personal plea and seeing the misery of the beggars than by being coerced by law. Therefore suppose that beggars in a certain city are able to obtain an amount of one hundred through pleas and personal supplications. If the legal system formalized almsgiving by listing the citizens and imposing fixed contributions on them, the official registrar would display an amount of barely forty. For citizens are as horrified at the idea of having to register for the sake of almsgiving as they are at the prospect of having to pay taxes. Perhaps we are allowed to deduce what might happen in other places from what has happened in this city, which is most generous toward the poor—and I do not mean to insult anyone else by saying that. Only half the amount of alms is recorded in the official register; therefore much less than anyone could ever have expected from a city in which the alms used to be most generous. Before three months had passed, a good part of that

---

[28] Ed. note: In ch. 11, concl. 1, p. 96.

registered sum had already been withdrawn. How much remains at this time, I do not know.

Let me now begin to secure the path that I will follow in response to the objections. In other regions, people have greater regard for other citizens,[29] and they can be compelled more easily by law to further the common good. Since it was in such a place that this method of almsgiving was decreed, I say truly that nobody can propose it as an example for the Spaniards to imitate.[30]

Mite Boxes

Regarding the amount of money which is collected in mite boxes placed in the churches, it will suffice to say how little it is, and less than all estimates. For even those who show mercy and generosity whenever they meet beggars on their way will forget to put alms into the boxes if they no longer come across poor people. When they enter a church, they do not give as much to a mute stone or piece of wood as they would give to a living human being. That is why those offering boxes are so void of funds that no name could suit them less than the name "treasure boxes."[31]

Moreover, only the heads of families[32] are enrolled in the official register. But when beggars are allowed to roam about, perhaps the wife will pay something if the husband gives nothing, for wives show more willingness toward the poor. If the father does not give alms, the son will. What the master might not have contributed, the servant will grant him.

---

[29] *populares magis sunt atque civiles.*

[30] Ed. note: Soto refers to the legislation in towns such as Ypres and Wittenberg.

[31] *gazophylacia.* Ed. note: The etymology of the Greek word γαζοφυλάκιον (offering box, but literally "treasure-keeper") implies that the boxes contain treasure, i.e., that they are filled rather than mostly empty. The word is used in the story of the widow's mite in Mark 12:41–44 and Luke 21:1–4.

[32] *patresfamilias.*

Alms Consisting of Household Goods

But the argument which possesses the most strength in this affair is the following: alms usually do not consist of money alone but of every kind of good from the household. For you can find people who are too frugal to give away money but are fine with their wife handing over a loaf of bread, the leftovers of the table, worn-out clothing, linen undergarments, a well-trodden shoe, or a bundle of wood. Of course, if you remove these from the supply of alms—something which cannot be avoided if we follow their plan—I do not know whether you could still receive half the amount.

But besides discussing the detrimental reduction in almsgiving, which undoubtedly follows from this plan to confine the poor, we can tackle this topic in a different way.

The Essence of Mercy

The essence of mercy does not lie only in everyone bringing aid and assistance to the poor but additionally, and indeed most of all, in the inner soul which feels compassion for a poor man and pity because of his misfortune. When his means are insufficient to perform an actual good work, his affection will be numbered among his merits before God. We can observe this in Christ. As we read in Matthew and Mark,[33] before he extinguished the hunger of that multitude in the wasteland and took away their tiredness by reinvigorating them, he felt pity for that multitude which had been with him for three days. From this divine affection an external work proceeded.

So those who whisk away the poor from the eyes of the Christians take away, as people say, the most delicious cream contained in the outstanding virtue of mercy. For just as men cannot be courageous and unwavering unless they have been frequently provoked by the sight of armed enemies, so they can only be merciful if they have seen the hardships, misfortunes, and adversities of the poor with their own eyes and have reflected on them. Even though the sight of poor people causes nausea for some people—whose ears are deafened by the

---

[33] Ed. note: Matt. 15:32–39; Mark 8:1–9.

lamentations of beggars—there are others with a more lenient character in this regard who soften their hearts enough to show mercy when they are confronted with the hardships of the poor. They lower the feathers which they normally put proudly on their cap (on account of their noble lineage, honor, and good fortune) when confronted with people of the same human species who have encountered such a different fate and who are down on their luck. They realize that in this life, they could have been in a position similar or even equal to that of beggars, and that in the future eternal happiness, they will perhaps be in an inferior rank to them.

Who can doubt that the sight of the poor and their lamentations during the principal church festivals and especially during the Holy Week moves the souls of Christians so intensely that it incites them to show mercy and makes them want to experience the Passion of Christ? At any rate, I encountered people last year who said with some sadness that a Passion Week without the lamentations of poor people would grow silent, like a religious festival celebrated without music.

Last but not least, Greatest Prince, is it not of the utmost importance that we teach the youth from the start of their education to show mercy? We would follow the example of that holiest of men, Job, who thought that the basis of his virtuousness lay therein: that his mercy had grown with him from his infancy.[34] In what way can a boy be instructed in that most sacred virtue without seeing or hearing the misfortunes of the poor with his own senses? Those who are now diligently managing[35] the alms of the poor have seen the miseries of the poor with their own eyes, and hence are able to be merciful and compassionate toward the poor. Supposing these institutions that confine the poor remain in place for a century, those who are born now will never see beggars at the entrance of their house, nor will they go out to visit confined beggars. What feelings toward the poor could such people have?

---

[34] Job 31:18.

[35] *procurant*. Ed. note: Different reading in the Spanish version of 1545. Soto, *Relecciones y opúsculos*, II-2, 337: "*Por esso, los que agora tratan destos artículos son tan misericordiosos, porque han visto pobres.*"

But not only for the previous reason do we have a religious duty to provide the poor in their presence with aid and support, but certainly also in honor and obedience to Christ. There is a passage in Paul's letter to Timothy in which Paul teaches and encourages us to do works of mercy such as "to wash the feet of the saints and to come to the aid of those undergoing great suffering."[36] In his fourteenth homily, Chrysostom commented on this passage, saying that we have to exhibit works of mercy to the poor in person and that we have to do it with remarkable eagerness, a complete willingness in our soul and the greatest alacrity and devotion, as if we were performing those works for Christ himself.[37] For as Chrysostom wrote, we should not delegate our works for the poor to our servants or maids but apply ourselves to the poor. We should obey the following words of Christ: "If I have washed your feet, as your Lord and Master"—it is as if he had said, "I have allowed no one else to do this humble work"—"then you have to wash each other's feet as well."[38] And Chrysostom added that even someone stationed in the highest honor, whose renowned house shone brightly with glory, would still not be as superior to the poor as Christ was to his disciples. When you serve a poor person, you serve Christ. For Christ said, "He who has received an infant in my name, has received me."[39] And "insofar as you have done something for one of these little ones, you have done it for me."[40] So far Chrysostom. That is why we have to fear that Christ will reveal to us on the last day that he has lived among us as a beggar, and that he will reproach us for having closed our eyes to the poor. For we rarely read of church prelates or very famous men that were saints without any historical record stating that they personally gave food to the poor or even touched their wounds with their own hands. Leaving others

---

[36] 1 Tim. 5:10.

[37] Chrysostom, *Homilia XIV in epistulam primam ad Timotheum* 2 (PG 62:573).

[38] John 13:14.

[39] Matt. 18:5.

[40] Matt. 25:40.

unmentioned for the moment, I want to tell the Son of the Emperor about an empress: the history of the Most Holy Empress Flaccilla, wife of Theodosius. She is showered with honors in the *Tripartite History*, especially because of the following:

> Even though she was at the top of the royal pyramid, her greatest concern under the imperial purple was for the lame and the feeble. She was not helped by servants or other aides, but acted by herself. She went to their dwellings and provided each one with what he needed. Running through the guesthouses of churches in a similar manner, she served the infirm with her own hands; she cleaned their pots, tasted their broth, offered them spoons, broke bread, served them food, washed their goblets, and did all the work which servants and maids are accustomed to perform solemnly.[41]

For the Christians of antiquity permanently bore in mind the words that Christ said he would speak at the last day, when he will confirm that he has been among us naked and a stranger, hungry, and suffering from thirst.[42] He did so to ensure that we would always receive the poor as if each and every one of them were Christ himself, that we would take care of them with works of humility and rejoice when we see them.

We discussed these things for the sake of those who have a kind disposition toward the poor and who thereby cannot bear their absence without difficulty. But we also did it for those inhumane men who refuse to listen to the requests of the poor because they are greedy and have hearts of stone. It is beneficial to confront them with the sight of beggars. For I hear some people, in fact Christian and pious men, adducing the following argument among others in favor of this institution for the confinement of the poor: if some foreigner or pagan would see men in our midst begging out of extreme poverty, he would accuse us of cruelty and inhumanity. Furthermore, our religion would become an object of reproach for him.

---

[41] Cassiodorus, *Historia ecclesiastica tripartita* VII.31 (PL 69:1147–48).

[42] Ed. note: Matt. 25:35–36, 42–43.

However, if he would observe that the poor have been put away, concealed, and prohibited from leaving, and that they have not been fed more lavishly and treated with greater expense by us than what this method of almsgiving allows for, perhaps we might hear worse things from him.

In any event, I take a different approach. Even in a republic of Christians there will inevitably be people who are merciless and cruel toward the poor. May there always be beggars in their presence. For even if beggars are unable to convince them to be compassionate, they can at least denounce their injustice on the day of judgment. Is this not what Christ taught when he told us about that rich glutton who dressed in purple and fine linen and feasted splendidly on a daily basis?[43] He was not being tormented in hell for refusing to give alms to a beggar far away from him, but because he had shown no mercy at all to Lazarus, despite being rich and seeing that pauper lying in front of his gate, sore-ridden and hoping to satisfy his hunger from the crumbs which fell from a copious table. Look at how many things Christ adds to his example to increase the guilt and shame of that rich person. For he added that the dogs, to which the rich man had given the crumbs, were more merciful toward the poor man than the rich man, because they at least licked his sores.

Therefore, Christ needs beggars lying at the gates of cruel, rich people that they may witness against them on the day of judgment, accusing them and putting them to shame.

The Gates of the Prelates

In contrast, how wonderful is that crowd of poor people at the gates of prelates and magnates who are kind and merciful! They are relieved by their benefactors, and they heap praises on them and commend them in their prayers to God. Perhaps there are some deviant men among them, but even so, many of them will be righteous and therefore

---

[43] Luke 16:19–31.

able, according to that saying of our Lord, to receive us into the eternal dwellings.44

If kings and glorious emperors still imitate the example of Christ by washing the feet of poor men once a year and by serving at their tables, why then would it not be laudable and honorable for poor people standing at the gates of other great and noble men to partake daily in their meals?

If Gregory, Ambrose, and Augustine, those holy fathers and kings of the church, heard that the houses of princes and bishops were not open for Christ's beggars, and that they were not admitted inside for a meal, they would certainly not assess and condemn it differently than if they had heard that children were being denied access to the houses of their fathers. We read of Gregory that he never sat at his table without poor people or foreigners by his side, and that his house was frequently visited by beggars.45 On account of his works for the poor, he became so well deserving that angels under the guise of paupers often accepted his alms and sat at his table among his poor guests.

King Louis of France

But let us mention another most renowned individual, both in terms of ancestry and piety, in addition to the Highest Pontiff. I am speaking of King Louis IX of France who is on his own merits rightfully counted among the saints. He was the son of Blanche of Castile, a descendant of the kings of Spain. By no means can I be led to believe that he would have ever ordered that confinement of beggars or even approved of it. As a consequence of his upbringing by his mother, he had the following habit: On the occasion of church festivals, he served food with his own hand to more than two hundred poor people before he himself would begin to eat. Each day they received abundant meals in the royal palace. Every Saturday, he washed their feet with his own

---

44 Ed. note: Luke 16:9.

45 Ed. note: Ioannes Diaconus, *Sancti Gregorii Magni Vita* III, 23 (PL 75:96–97).

hands, wiped them dry, and kissed them. Afterwards, he gave them extraordinarily large alms.

The Plan Is Too Novel

For all these reasons, I cannot imagine how this plan to prohibit the poor from begging could be commended on the basis of its antiquity, which is alleged by the plan's authors. Indeed, the plan gets shattered particularly by one of the most important counterarguments: it is a novel invention just like the plan to expel foreigners, which has never been known to either pagans or the early Christians. For if it had deserved a place among the laws of mercy, the church fathers would have put it in writing for us a long time ago. I will explain this further in the next chapter where I will refute the reasons and arguments which the authors of this plan advance.

12

Weighing the Reasons and Arguments to Prohibit the Poor from Begging

The authors of the policy that consists in confining beggars have attempted to base their opinion on a first principle, the divine word in Deuteronomy 15: "There will be no pauper or beggar among you, that the Lord may bless you in the land which he will give you in possession."[1]

Saint Thomas refuted this argument saying that "this legal precept does not prohibit anyone from begging, but prohibits the rich from being so stingy that they force some to beg out of poverty."[2] That response should be kept in mind in order to correctly understand all other texts which say something on this subject, such as church statutes and rules laid down by the saints. After all, nowhere on earth have the poor been prevented from begging. The rich, on the other hand, must refrain from forcing the poor into begging by their own cruelty.

---

[1] Deut. 15:4.

[2] Thomas Aquinas, *Summa theologiae* II-2, q. 187, a. 5, obj. 3.

The Term "Beggar"[3]

Let us add here that, contrary to what many people believe, the meaning of the word "beggar" not only comprises someone who walks from house to house to ask for alms but anyone who is so needy that he has to live on daily alms and gifts. Even though he receives them at home, he is still considered a beggar in the proper sense.

While a poor person is someone who has his own means to live his life, however difficult and miserable it is, a beggar has no means of his own, living merely on what he receives from others. To beg is not only to ask for alms but also to receive what is spontaneously offered.[4] Albeit not so explicitly, this is not only taught by Saint Thomas in the passage which we have just cited but also by Chrysostom, or whoever the author of the *Imperfectum* was, when he commented on Matthew: "Blessed are the poor in spirit."[5] According to the author, the Greek text does not say "the poor" but "the beggars."[6]

Therefore, the passage in Deuteronomy not only reminds the people that there should be no beggars asking for alms by going from door to door but also that there should be no one still in need of daily alms and food rations while being confined at home. Yet the latter category of people is created by these articles. Therefore, the authors of the articles should not believe that they have adequately met the requirements of that precept from Deuteronomy. It was not a precept on pain of mortal sin but an exhortation to practice charity which has to abound among all decent people. That is why subsequent to the exhortation, the chapter in Deuteronomy goes on to say that the poor will always be there.[7] Something similar can be found in the Gospels: as often as Christ taught us to show mercy and urged us to give alms,

---

[3] *mendicus*. Ed. note: For the meaning of the term "vagabond" (*vagabundus*), see ch. 3, p. 18.

[4] Ps.-Chrysostom, *Opus imperfectum in Matthaeum*, hom. 9.5 (PG 56:680).

[5] Ed. note: Matt. 5:3.

[6] Ed. note: οἱ πτωχοί.

[7] Deut. 15:11.

he nevertheless foretold the harshness of our hearts, saying, "You will always have the poor with you."[8]

The Second Argument

Second, they take Paul as an example for their policy plans, supposedly because he organized similar collections in Macedonia and Galatia. He mentions them in his letter to the Romans[9] and in his first letter to the Corinthians.[10]

But those two collections, as Saint Thomas interprets them,[11] were organized for a very different reason. Not that the words of Paul needed an interpreter. For the matter is so transparent by itself. For these collections of alms did not take place to help and relieve the poor of the same city in which they took place. According to the Acts of the Apostles, the story goes as follows: A very severe famine spread through Jerusalem and surrounding Judea.[12] Paul and Barnabas were therefore sent to Macedonia and Achaia in order to preach and request aid for the Christians in Jerusalem and Judea, especially for those who had devoted themselves to preaching and divine worship. This is what Paul outlined in his letter to the Galatians: "James, Cephas[13] and John gave me and Barnabas their hands in fellowship, that we should go to the gentiles, and they to the circumcised. They only asked us to remain mindful of the poor, but I had been eager to do that all along."[14] What the Macedonians and Galatians collected was carried to Jerusalem by the apostles themselves. The apostle attests to this in his letter to the Romans when he says, "From here I will go to Jerusalem to minister to the saints. For the Macedonians and Achaians agreed to raise some

---

[8] Ed. note: Matt. 26:11; Mark 14:7; John 12:8.

[9] Rom. 15:25–31.

[10] 1 Cor. 16:1–4.

[11] Thomas Aquinas, *In primam epistolam ad Corinthios*, ch. 16, lec. 1.

[12] Acts 11:27–30.

[13] Ed. note: That is, Peter.

[14] Gal. 2:9–10.

funds for the poor saints in Jerusalem. It pleased them, since they were their debtors. After all, if the gentiles have been permitted to partake in their spiritual goods, they should also share their own carnal goods with them."[15] Observe what an extremely effective thing these collections were for the relief of the saints who served the gospel. He persuaded the Corinthians just like he did the Macedonians, writing, "Concerning the collections which take place for the benefit of the saints [i.e., the saints in Jerusalem], follow the arrangements which I have made in the churches of Galatia." Paul also added the correct method: "On every first day of the week [i.e. on every Sunday], every one of you has to set aside and store as much as is pleasing to him, that the collections do not have to take place when I come [i.e. to carry what has been collected to Jerusalem]."[16] Those alms were therefore not collected to prevent the poor from begging.

Before I touch upon a different subject, let me not pass over something else which Chrysostom noted in his interpretation of this passage in his forty-third homily.[17] He said that every Christian should draw inspiration from this example and devote a little box for the poor at home in the place where he usually prays. Just like a priest who first washes his hands before offering the sacrifice, he should put alms in the box before praying that he may be clean when he goes to pray. For it is written: "Give alms, and see, all things are clean unto you."[18]

The Third Argument

The third argument which they invoke for their plan is the following: that there were no beggars going from door to door to ask for alms in the early church. However, this argument would carry us unto a truly vast field where there is much worthy of mention. First of all, as I just

---

[15] Rom. 15:25–27.

[16] 1 Cor. 16:1–2.

[17] Chrysostom, *In epistulam primam ad Corinthios Homilia* 43.4 (PG 61:372).

[18] Ed. note: Luke 11:41.

said, we cannot find anything in the Acts of the Church[19] or in the writings of any holy father from which we could deduce that the freedom of the poor to go beg wherever they please was ever taken away.

Second, nobody can dispute that there were poor beggars at the time of Christ, our Savior. On the one hand, he cured large multitudes of poor, lame, and blind people, or people suffering from sickness and weariness, from which we can deduce that there were very many beggars who wandered through the streets. On the other hand, it seems obvious that the following advice of Christ in Luke 14 refers to beggars: "When you make lunch or dinner, do not invite your friends ... nor your rich neighbors. But invite the poor, the feeble, the lame, and the blind, and you will be blessed."[20]

To make sure nobody uses the sophistry that says that "they were living in confinement," observe what follows immediately: the parable of the man who held a large dinner.[21] When the invitees declined to come, he told his slaves, "Go out into the streets and squares of the city."[22] Not only that, but also, "Go out into the highways and hedges, and bring the poor, the feeble, the blind, and the lame here."[23] For beggars are in the habit of sitting in such places in the city and at crossroads. Does the book of Acts not contain the story of a lame person who was carried each day to the gate of the temple to ask for alms, and whom Peter, having no money with him, ordered to stand up and walk?[24] And the Gospel of John tells us about a beggar whose sight was restored by Christ: "His neighbors, and those who had seen him begging before, asked, 'Is this the same man?,'" etc.[25] The words "those who had seen him begging before" imply that he usually begged in public.

---

[19] Ed. note: i.e., the Acts of the Apostles.

[20] Luke 14:12–14.

[21] Luke 14:16–24.

[22] Luke 14:21.

[23] Luke 14:21, 23.

[24] Ed. note: Acts 3:1–6.

[25] Ed. note: John 9:8.

There were beggars not only at the time of Christ. Augustine also bears witness to their presence in his "Sermon on the Second Sunday of Advent" and frequently in other works. In this sermon, he preached that Christians are obliged to give more generous alms: "On the occasion of the church festivals we should, to the best of our ability, give more generously. Above all, we should invite the poor more frequently for dinner."[26] He was of course talking about beggars who were accustomed to being allowed into the houses of the rich to feast with them.

Mendicancy was at that time so common that many Christians sold their possessions out of piety and humility, distributed them among the poor, and lowered themselves to that humblest of conditions, as we have seen in the previous chapter.[27] In a matter established beyond reasonable doubt, there is no need for supplementary witnesses. For the accounts of all writers that have handed down the deeds of the holy fathers bear witness to the fact that there have always been beggars in the church and that the mendicant orders did not take their name in combination with the practice itself from somewhere else.

As a third consideration, I would like to add here that in the early church (namely, until the time of Gregory and even longer), the piety of Christians was something else and indeed very different. Different were the dispositions of Christians toward the poor; different were their institutions; and different from today were the outcomes of their poor relief policy intended to free the poor from the burden of having to ask for alms.

The authors of these articles referred to what is written in the *Life of Pope Clement*, namely, that he kept a written record of the names of poor people from every region and did not allow anyone whom he had cleansed through the sanctification of baptism to be subjected to the state of mendicancy. Similar words can be cited in the *Deeds* of Sylvester, Gregory,[28] Martin, and all other fathers from that era. But

---

[26] Ps.-Augustine, *Sermo 116 De adventu domini II*, 4 (PL 39:1976).

[27] Ed. note: Soto is referring to the beginning of ch. 11 (pp. 93–94), where he speaks about Saints Alexius, Arsenius, and Fabiola. In some versions of the 1547 edition, these examples are inserted for a second time into the main text.

[28] Ioannis Diaconus, *Sancti Gregorii Magni Vita* II.30 (PL 75:98).

the authors of the current plan should pay attention to the way in which they stopped those poor people from begging. They did not introduce a law to prohibit them from begging or to forcefully keep them confined. So in what manner did they stop them? By keeping a written record of the names of the poor and by sending them ample rations, making sure that they no longer needed to beg. Only following this most pious course of action did they take away their right to beg. If citing all relevant legal sources would not be tedious for the reader, I would cite them now and explain everything at length. However, I suggest you read the titles "On religious homes" in the *Decretals*[29] and the *Clementines*,[30] and you will clearly understand how much care for the poor was entrusted to the prelates. These passages will also show you with how much concern and solicitude those illustrious priests, like true fathers, looked after the interests of their poor sons and managed and supported them at their own expense.

Different Kinds of Hospices

Besides the personal alms which were given individually, a great effort was made to construct different kinds of hospices in all places, as is evident from the law *Sancimus*[31] in the Code of Justinian, to which reference is made in canon *Tributum*.[32] There were *xenodochia*, which are guesthouses for the poor; *orphanotrophia*, which were shelters for orphans; *ptochotrophia*, in which the poor and the beggars were fed; *brephotrophia*, a house in which infants were nursed; and *gerontocomia*, a place where the elderly and weak found relief. The church back then was still sharpened by the freshness of Christ's recently shed blood and flourished thanks to its kindness and compassion toward the poor. In fact, no other method worked better to win over the souls of men and draw them to faith in Christ. That is why Julian the Apostate, who declared open war on the church, went to great lengths to encourage

---

[29] Dec. Greg. 3.36.1–9.

[30] Clem. 3.11.1–2.

[31] Cod. 1.2.22.

[32] Dec. Grat. C.23 q.8 c.22–23.

the pagans to build, endow, and finance *xenodochia* and hospices for the poor, as is written in the *Ecclesiastical History*.[33] He wanted the pagans to surpass the Christians in compassion that they might retain the pagans who were hastening toward Christianity.

But why do we vie with the example of that church which helped the poor so well that they no longer had to ask for alms? A fourth of all the yields and revenues of that church were set aside and allocated to the support of the poor, as can be seen in the decrees of Gelasius,[34] of Simplicius,[35] and of the Council of Toledo,[36] all of which have been included in Gratian's *Decretum*. And even though the poor were already helped in such an excellent way, nowhere do we read that begging was forbidden to them. What reason then can we adduce in our times—wishing to be given the charity of that people, the prelates of that era, the laws of that church, and finally its allocation of yearly incomes to the poor—I repeat, what reason can we adduce to keep beggars from their right and liberty to ask for alms?

I will not reply to that council of the ecclesiastical province of Cologne, for it did not have the force of papal authority and did not properly decree anything on the matter beyond what stems from common law.[37] Neither can the people of Cologne, Ypres, or the Germans generally serve as examples for the Spanish in this affair. Beyond the fact that they have a greater sense of public responsibility,[38] as we mentioned earlier,[39] their public revenues are much larger, allowing them to allocate just amounts of relief to the poor. We can observe this in the statutes of Cologne and Ypres, and it is also commonly said of Venice, Genoa, and many other cities. But I do not see how we who only obtain funds through begging could provide enough support to

---

[33] Sozomen, *Historia ecclesiastica* VI. Ed. note: i.e., V.16 (PG 67:1261–64).

[34] Dec. Grat. C.12 q.2 c.27.

[35] Dec. Grat. C.12 q.2 c.28.

[36] Dec. Grat. C.12 q.2 c.31.

[37] *iura communia*.

[38] *magis politici*.

[39] See ch. 11, pp. 105–6.

the poor to be able to lawfully keep them from begging—as well considered as these laws of almsgiving might be.

What has been weighing on my mind more than anything else is that the legitimate proposers, promulgators, and executors of these laws and regulations should not be laypeople but priests and prelates of the church. For where in Sacred Scripture or the sacred canons has the office of patron of the poor been assigned to laypersons? Where have priests or bishops of the church, who are like the fathers of the poor, not been chosen for this duty? Nowhere. Because Christ wanted his priests, as his disciple Paul says, to be free from the cares of laypeople. "He who is without a wife," as Paul says, "is concerned about the things which are the Lord's—how he may please God. But he who has a wife, is concerned about the things which are of the world—how to please his wife—and he is divided."[40] Why am I saying all this? Do you think that I want to close my eyes to the fact that the office and care for the poor cannot, in the end, remain in the hands of laypeople, even if they are wise and honest men? It is simply not according to the order of things as willed by God and the church. Since the building which we want to construct is spiritual in nature, the bishops should be its architects. The task of the people is to supply the wood and materials.[41] For laypeople marry wives, have families, and are heavily involved in other tasks, trades, and concerns. They can hardly disentangle themselves from these in order to have enough time to spare for those offices of mercy. Unless some alms for the poor are set aside in order to pay them a wage and compensate them for their efforts, you can hardly find persons who retain their office. What we see happen in practice is that the poor are cheated out of a considerable part of their alms because it is allotted to administrators. But you may object that today's prelates do not care for the poor as much as their predecessors did. I acknowledge that, but I cannot put my hope in laypeople acting like bishops. I do not believe that they will make it possible to sustain the poor in perpetual confinement by sufficiently fulfilling their duty and

---

[40] Ed. note: 1 Cor. 7:32–33.

[41] Ed. note: The "wood and materials" are the alms for the poor, as can be derived from the Spanish text. Soto, *Relecciones y opúsculos*, II-2, 357.

by compensating all the injury done. At the moment, those who have assumed this duty are noblemen of the highest rank, very Christian in their disposition, who are able to continue the undertaking for the time being. But afterwards others will succeed them in this office, so it is inevitable that the quality of the work will gradually start to decline and break down.

Epilogue

But since I am already steering my ship to the port, I want to lower the sails. Therefore, I call to witness that which carries the most weight in everything that people try to undertake: experience. This new method of almsgiving has been in common use already for about three years. Make sure that you, Most Prudent Prince, know what fruits this method has produced in actual practice. Since that is not a matter of law but, as people say, of facts, I am not competent to judge. Yet in my experience and based on what I hear and see in this city and what I similarly infer from other places, there is much that speaks against this undertaking. But since you perceive such things very easily, make an effort to obtain the true answers to the following questions:

First, crowds of able-bodied beggars have been expelled from the large cities. Have there been among them some legitimate poor who were indiscriminately forced to leave?

Second, perhaps we do not see any beggar passing through the streets. Does this mean that the number of poor persons in the old hospices has increased, or has the number of hospices increased in which those who used to roam are received?

Third, are there Christians complaining about the fact that there are no longer beggars using force to extort alms from them? For in this regard, it is customary for "the Kingdom of God to suffer violence"[42] as well.

Fourth, some alms have been preserved because the vagabonds have been expelled. Did these alms go entirely to the locals and to those who were too ashamed to ask for alms—which we should regard as

---

[42] Ed. note: Matt. 11:12.

the principal[43] goal of this effort? Or has their situation not improved at all, or only a little bit, while the total amount of alms which used to be collected became smaller?

Perhaps you observe that the undertaking progresses favorably, namely, that the alms do not become smaller in any way but become much larger and that the miseries, hardships, and misfortunes of the local poor, which oppress them heavily, are alleviated by the enlarged alms. In that case, invest great effort and assert your authority as a prince to make sure that the plan for these institutions goes forward. For in whatever direction we notice the mind of the prince leaning, thereto will all of us be inclined as well. That opinion is what we will applaud, support, and favor. All of us will defend, preach, and promote it.

But if you might sense that the undertaking has taken a turn for the worse, it would suffice to retain and praise the practices and arrangements which involve the registration of alms and serve to help and relieve poor residents suffering poverty at home. We should undertake every effort to make these arrangements succeed, for they can only be very much approved and appreciated by God. Other beggars, however, should retain their right to ask for alms. That a truly poor person undergoes public punishments for having begged is something which we will hopefully never hear said about a Christian kingdom where a most Christian prince reigns. Daniel explained the mystery of a strange statue to us:[44] even though it had a head of gold, a breast of silver, and the lowliest of feet, which were partly of iron and partly of clay, nevertheless when the feet were shattered, the body of precious metals immediately fell to the ground. What if the higher classes in a republic are also sustained by the lowliest class, the poor, on account of their merits in giving alms? Removing the poor from our midst puts the entire body at risk.

But I fear that you have begun to grow tired of this already lengthy discourse, for I seem to have been carried away by my enthusiasm, writing more than I had planned. Even if this humble work of mine has achieved nothing else, you will not regret reading at least some

---

[43] Ed. note: We read *precibus* as *praecipuus*.

[44] Dan. 2:31–45.

of its contents as you strive to acquire that most outstanding and illustrious virtue of mercy.

The will and mercy of God have gifted you with a great light which constitutes the hope of your kingdoms. Indeed, besides your father and very few people, nobody has ever been raised by nature with anything like it. How should you repay God for his amazing generosity if not through works of mercy? The virtues of justice and mercy should adorn the seat of the prince, just like the throne of God. The virtue of mercy, however, shines brighter in both God and king. We are elated at the position you rightly hold among mortals, but God willing, may you by means of both virtues make us rejoice in perpetuity when we see you in a similar position among the saints.

Vale.

Index

able-bodied beggars, 6, 24–25, 68–72, 75–76, 103, 124
Abraham, 35, 78, 79, 82–83
Acts of the Apostles, 96, 117–18, 119–20
Alexius, Saint, 94, 120n27
alms, almsgiving, 84–85, 88, 97, 107
  benefit to giver, 90–91
  collection of, xxxiv–xxxv, 102–6, 117–18
  definition, 77–78, 79–80
  as detrimental, 81–82
  duty to give, x, 7–8, 31, 59–62, 85–86
  reductions in, 102–5, 107, 123, 125
  right to beg, 30–33, 41–43, 85–86, 98–99, 101–2
  by subscription, taxes, xxx, xxxii, 99, 105
  withholding as mortal sin, 31, 61–63, 116
Ambrose, 22n28, 51, 60, 62–63, 80, 88, 112
Aquinas, Thomas, xi, xxvii–xxviii, xxix, 31, 60, 94, 115, 117
Aristotle, xvi–xvii, xxii, 20, 23, 50, 94, 97

Arsenius, Saint, 94, 120n27
Augustine, 15, 22, 64, 76, 112, 120
  mercy, 80–82
Authenticum "On the quaestor," 24, 28, 46

begging, beggars, xxiv, 29, 51, 93–94, 116–17, 123
  door to door, 6, 14, 118–19
  right to, 30–33, 41–43, 85–86, 98–99, 101–2
Beltrán de Heredia, Vicente, x–xi, xii, xiv, xv, xxvi–xxviin69, xxvii–xxviiiin74
body of Christ, 33–34, 59–60

Cano, Melchor, xv–xvi
canon law, 8–9, 15, 18, 22, 60, 62–63, 74, 82, 87, 121–22
Carranza, Bartolomé de, xii, xiv, xv–xvi
Carthage, Fifth Council of, 9
Castro, Alfonso de, xxv
Cervantes, Miguel de, xxiii
charity, bond of, 59–62
  order of, 42–43, 84
Charles V, xiii–xiv
Christ Jesus, 90–91, 103–4, 123

Index

body, 33–34, 59–60
  law of, 33–34
  poor and, 51–54, 55–56, 83–84, 107, 109–11
Chrysostom, John, xxxv, xlvii, 22, 88, 116
  poor, 51, 63–64, 72–74, 78–80, 109, 118
church, the
  bishops, vii, 32, 104–5, 112, 123–24
  early, 96, 117–18, 119–20
  poor and, xxxv, 40–41, 69, 106, 108, 120–21
  prelates, 111–12, 120–21, 123
Cicero, 20, 35, 50–51, 55n31, 93n2, 95n9
Cologne, 122
colonate, 24
colonialism, xiv, xx
common law, Roman, xxxiii, 18, 24–25, 28–29, 98, 122
confession of sin, 85–87, 88–89
Cyprian, 40–41

Daniel, prophet, 90, 125
David, King, 8, 53
Decalogue, xxii
Deliberación en la causa de los pobres, xxv–xxviii
  Latin edition, xxvii–xxviii, xlv–xlvii, 9
  Mexican manuscript (student notes), xxviii–xxix
Demetrius the Philosopher, 20–21
divine law, 19–20, 31, 36

Ecclesiasticus, 8, 21n23, 68, 75, 81–82, 90
Ennius, 55
examinations of poor, 78–80, 88–91

poor relief laws, ix–x, xxxii, xxxiv, 13, 49–50, 100–101
exile, 28, 30
Ezekiel, prophet, 22–23

Fabiola, Saint, 94, 120n27
false poor, xxxiv, 12, 22, 43–44, 47, 54–56, 67–68
Flaccilla, Empress, 110
foreign beggars, xxiii, xxxiii, 11–13, 47, 100–101, 119–20
  exclusion of, 39–40, 43
  expulsion of, 14, 28, 30, 33, 34, 37
  freedom of movement, 27, 40–43
  hospitality to, 35–37
  plagues and, 43–44
fraternal correction, 77–79, 81–82, 87, 89–90
fraud, theft, 62–64, 74–76, 101–2

Germany, Germans, xiii, xxiii, 122
Giginta, Miguel, xxx
gratitude, 55–56
Gregory the Great, 7–8, 112, 120
Gregory XIII, Pope, xvi

hatred of the poor, 45, 51–52, 54–55, 68, 100
Henry II, King, 28–29
honor, xxxii, 14, 103
  of poor, 51–54, 80, 88–89, 112
Horace, 21
hospices, 14, 31, 93, 97, 102, 121–24
hospitality, xxxiii, 78–80, 82
  to foreigners, 35–37
  right of, 35–37, 45–46
hostels, guesthouses, 101–2, 110
human natural inclinations, xx–xxii, xxxiii
Hurtado de Mendoza, Diego, xii, xiii, xxvi

Index

idleness, 19–23
Inquisition, the, xv–xvi
Isaiah, prophet, 63–64
Isidore, 8
ius commune, 18
ius gentium (law of nations), xx–xxii, xxxiii

Jerome, 22, 62, 94
Jerusalem, 22–23, 46, 96
  collection for, 117–18
Jesus Christ. *See* Christ Jesus
Job, 8, 79, 83, 108
John, apostle, 60–61
judgment, day of, 62–64, 109–10, 111–12
Julian the Apostate, 122
justice, x, 11, 68–69, 77–78, 89–90, 98–99
Justinian, Emperor, 24–25
  Code of, vii, 24, 70, 121
  Digest of, 17–18, 30, 98
  Novels of, 24, 28, 46

law, 17, 28–29
  of Christ, 33–34
  divine, 19–20, 31, 36
  of nations, xx–xxii, xxxiii, 30, 46, 63
  natural, xx–xxii, 18, 20–21, 30–31, 34, 95–96
  See also canon law; Roman law
laziness, xxi. *See also* idleness
legitimate poor, 12, 29–30, 47, 50, 56, 70, 103, 124
León, Luis de, xxii
leyes de Toro, 29
Louis IX, King of France, 112–13
love for poor, xxxv, 95–96, 97
Lutheranism, xii, xv
Luther, Martin, vii

Madrid, xxiii–xxiv, 12, 25, 29
Medina, Bartolomé de, xxii
Medina, Juan de, Benedictine monk. *See* Robles, Juan de
Medina, Juan de, theologian at Alcalá, xxv
mendicant religious orders, 20, 52–53, 93–94, 96, 105, 120
Mendoza, Diego Hurtado de, xii, xiii, xxvi
mercy, ix–x, xxxii–xxxiii, 51, 62, 69, 77–82, 126
  definition, 84–85, 107–11
  duty of, 83–84, 85–86
  for enemies, sinners, 80–82, 84
México, Biblioteca Nacional de, xxviii–xxix
morality, ethics, xix–xx, xxxi, xxxiv
moral reform, xxxiv, 73–74
  fraternal correction, 77–79, 81–82, 87, 89–90
moral theology, xxv, xxxi
mortal sin, 31, 61–63, 116

Native Americans, xiv, xx
natural inclinations, xx–xxii, xxxiii
natural law, xx–xxii, 18, 20–21, 30–31, 34, 95–96
natural rights, xxxiii
Nicholas of Myra, 56, 88
noble poor, 14, 71–72
Nueva Recopilación, xlvi, 11–13, 25, 28–29, 70

Ordenamiento, 25, 28–29, 70

Paris, University of, 39
Paul III, Pope, xiii
Paul, apostle, 17, 52, 109, 123
  body of Christ, 33–34
  giving, 31, 35, 42–43, 79, 91

129

Index

idleness, 19–20
Jerusalem collection, 117–18
peasants, 24
Pelagius I, Pope, 40–41
Philip II of Spain, 3–4, 5–9
pilgrims, pilgrimage, xxiv, 18, 45–46
   care for, 100–101
   Way of Santiago, xxiv, 13, 45–47
Plato, 22, 35
poor, the, xxxv
   able-bodied, 6, 24–25, 68–72, 75–76, 103, 124
   condition improvement, 101–2
   confining, concealing, 32, 51, 97–99, 102, 107–11, 112, 116, 125
   crime, 89–90
   examinations of, 78–80, 88–91
   false, xxxiv, 12, 22, 43–44, 47, 54–56, 67–68
   fraudulent, 72–74, 104
   gratitude, 55–56
   hatred for, 45, 51–52, 54–55, 68, 100
   injustice, 68–69
   legitimate, 12, 29–30, 47, 50, 56, 70, 103, 124
   love for, xxxv, 95–96, 97
   of noble blood, 14, 71–72
   See also foreign beggars
poor relief laws, ix–x, xxii–xxiv, 83
   alms, central collection of, xxxiv–xxxv, 102–6, 117–18
   confession requirement, 85–87, 88–89
   examinations, ix–x, xxxii, xxxiv, 13, 49–50, 100–101
   license, permission to beg, xxiv, 13, 98
   reductions in alms, 102–5, 107, 123, 125
   registration, 88–89, 105, 106

Zamora, xxv–xxvi, 14–15
praetors, 14, 41, 68–69, 83–84
prelates, 111–12, 120–21, 123
princes, 21, 30–32, 52–53, 94–95, 125–26
property, xxi–xxii
Pythagoras, 15, 95

rich, the
   alms, 42–43, 53–54, 55–56
   confession requirement, 85–86
   fraud, theft of, 62–64, 74–76, 101–2
   morals, sins of, xxxiv, 88–90
   poor and, 32–35, 51–52, 95–96, 99–100, 111, 115
   as stewards, 59–61, 64–65
rights, xxxiii
   to beg, 30–33, 41–43, 85–86, 98–99, 101–2
   of hospitality, 35–37, 45–46
   of religion, 45–46
Robles, Juan de, xxv, xxx, xxxii
Roman law, xxxiii, 17–18, 24–25, 28, 30, 46, 70, 98, 121–22

Salamanca, University of, viii, xi, xiv, xxvi, 9, 14
Santiago de Compostela (Way of Santiago), xxiv, 13, 45–47
scholastic theologians, 61–62
Seneca, 20–21, 22
Sepúlveda, Juan Ginés de, xiv
Sermon on the Mount, 52–53
Siete Partidas, 24–25
Socrates, 95–96
Solomon, King, 7, 21, 23, 59
Soto, Domingo de
   alms, xxvii–xxviii, 15
   life of, x–xvi
   morality, ethics, xix–xx, xxxi, xxxiv

natural law, inclinations, xx–xxii
poor laws, xxv–xxviii
property, xxi–xxii
Salamanca, University of, viii, xi, xiv, xxvi, 9
theology, xvii–xiv
Trent, Council of, xi–xii, xvii–xviii
works, xvi–xxii
Zamora, poor laws of, xxv–xxvi, 14–15
Spain, 33
  Córdoba, xxiii
  Inquisition, the, xv–xvi
  Madrid, xxiii–xxiv, 12, 25, 29
  poor laws, xxiii–xxiv
  Toledo, xxiii, xxvi, 6n2, 33, 122
  West Indies, xiv
Spaniards, xxxi–xxxii, 88, 105–6, 122
state, the
  alms, x, xxx, xxxii–xxxiii, xxxiv–xxxv, 30–32, 56, 105
  poor, care for, 5–9, 13–14, 39–41, 94–95
  princes, 21, 30–32, 52–53, 94–95, 125–26

Theophrastus, 35
thieves, bandits, 22, 76
  rich as, 62–64, 74–76, 101–2
Thomas, Saint. *See* Aquinas, Thomas
Tobias, 83–84

Toledo, xxiii, xxvi, 6n2, 33, 122
Toro, Gabriel del, xxv
Tours, Second Council of, 40–42
Trent, Council of, xi–xii, xvii–xviii

vagabonds, 6, 12, 29, 68, 83–84
  definition, 18–20
  expulsion of, 14, 25, 28, 56, 70, 76
  pilgrims, false, 45–46
  servitude, forced, 24–25
Valladolid, xiv, xv–xvi, xviii, xxiii, 11–13, 15
Venice, xxvii, xlv–xlvi, 3–4, 46, 123
Vitoria, Francisco de, xi–xii
Vives, Juan Luis, xxiii, xxvii, xlvi, 54–57

Way of Santiago (Santiago de Compostela), xxiv, 13, 45–47
wealthy. *See* rich, the
welfare, state, ix, xxxiv–xxxv, 6n2
West Indies, xiv
Wisdom, Book of, 51–52
work, 19–20

Ypres, xxiii, xxvii, 39, 100, 106n30, 122–23

Zamora, poor laws of, xxv–xxvi, 14–15

Sources in Early Modern Economics, Ethics, and Law

Titles Available in the Second Series

On the Law of Nature: A Demonstrative Method
Niels Hemmingsen

On the Duty to Keep Faith with Heretics
Martinus Becanus

The Right Use of Moral Philosophy
Pierre de la Place

Deliberation on the Cause of the Poor
Domingo de Soto

Titles Available in the First Series

A Treatise on the Alteration of Money
Juan de Mariana

On the Law in General
Girolamo Zanchi

On Law and Power
Johannes Althusius

On Exchange and Usury
Thomas Cajetan

On Righteousness, Oaths, and Usury: A Commentary on Psalm 15
Wolfgang Musculus

On Exchange: An Adjudicative Commentary
Martín de Azpilcueta

A Treatise on Money
Luis de Molina

The Mosaic Polity
Franciscus Junius

Of the Law of Nature
Matthew Hale

On Sale, Securities, and Insurance
Leonardus Lessius